A SAINSBURY COOKBOOK

MARVELLOUS MEALS WITH MINCE

JOSCELINE DIMBLEBY

D1470859

CONTENTS

Published exclusively for J Sainsbury plc
Stamford House Stamford Street
London SE1 9LL
by Martin Books
a division of Woodhead–Faulkner (Publishers) Limited
Fitzwilliam House 32 Trumpington Street
Cambridge CB2 1QY

First published 1982
New enlarged edition 1985
Third impression 1987
Fourth impression 1988
Text © Josceline Dimbleby 1987
Photographs and illustrations © J Sainsbury plc 1987

Printed in Great Britain

THE AUTHOR

From the age of five Josceline's childhood was spent abroad, mostly in the Middle East and South America, so that at an early age she learned to appreciate a wide range of food. Discovering the great variety of mince dishes on her travels made her realise its great potential for the creative cookery which she loves.

Josceline's instinct has always been to create her own recipes, which results in varied and interesting dishes, but leading a very busy life herself she appreciates the value of advance preparation and simple methods.

She has written many cookery articles for the national press and has featured on television and radio. Her first cookery book, *A Taste of Dreams,* appeared in 1976, followed by *Puddings, Desserts and Savouries,* which won the André Simon Award for the best cookery book of 1979. She is currently the cookery correspondent of the *Sunday Telegraph.*

Marvellous Meals with Mince is the sixth of the nine books she has written for Sainsbury's so far. This new edition has given Josceline the chance to add many completely new recipes.

Josceline lives in London with her husband, journalist and broadcaster David Dimbleby, and their three children.

INTRODUCTION

'They dined on mince, and slices of quince,
Which they ate with a runcible spoon;
And hand in hand, on the edge of the sand,
They danced by the light of the moon.'

Edward Lear

All over the world there are overwhelmingly popular specialities made with minced meat. The Americans, of course, have their hamburgers, the Greeks have moussaka, the Mexicans their chilli con carne, the Italians have Bolognese sauce, the Swedish have meat loaf and the Germans meatballs and stuffed cabbage; even the French have steak tartare. In North Africa, the Middle East, Turkey, India and the Far East

there are countless tempting ways of cooking
minced meat. In fact, almost any country you
can think of has its own mince recipes which
have often become national dishes, and to give
us our due, even we English can boast of our
shepherd's pie, which, when well made, can be
delicious.

The universal popularity of mince must surely
be due to its enormous versatility. It need never
be dull and should be an inspiration for the
creative cook, as it provides endless possibilities
for imaginative and tasty dishes.

You can make so many varieties of meatballs

Hot Stuffed Avocados Gratinée (page 47)
Meat Loaf with Blue Cheese Filling (page 19)
Far Eastern Pie (page 15)

and rissoles; rich, wintery ones in a sauce or spicy ones which can be grilled on a barbecue during the summer, their tantalising aroma wafting into the warm air. Mince can make delicious sauces for rice or noodles, and can be used in fillings for pies of all kinds. It can be used as an enhancing stuffing for vegetables or meat, or the mince can itself be stuffed with a surprise filling. Mince makes tasty stews and hearty soups and it can be used to great effect in pâtés and meat loaves. In fact, as I have found in writing this book, the scope is enormous and there are always new ideas cropping up.

The many possible ways of cooking mince also add to its versatility. Producing quite different results, it can be fried, baked, roasted, poached, stewed, grilled and barbecued.

Exciting and definite flavouring is what mince cries out for and absorbs so well: it will really take on any character you give it. It combines excellently with all kinds of herbs, spices and sauces. Breadcrumbs are often added, not only as a 'stretcher' but as a lightener, too, and when soaked in milk they help produce smooth and soft-textured meatballs. Cheese blends beautifully with mince and can either be incorporated into the mixture or used as a sauce. Certain vegetables, too, are especially good; onions and garlic are invaluable, tomatoes would be hard to do without. Dishes such as stuffed cabbage leaves and chilli con carne have proved that cabbage and kidney beans both mingle particularly well with mince. I have found that a purée of swede or celeriac is an interesting change to mashed potato on top of a shepherd's pie. Chopped spinach can add both moisture and flavour. There is always some new combination to try, which more often than not, because mince is such a chameleon, is a success.

Yet another virtue of mince is, of course, economy. What with stuffing, toppings, crusts and the addition of breadcrumbs, potatoes or rice, it can be invaluable when you are feeding an indeterminate number of people. When I am unsure of how many people are coming to a meal I invariably buy some mince, because it can nearly always be stretched to feed one or two last-minute guests or children's friends.

I often think that good bread is a better accompaniment to mince than potatoes or rice, and it also simplifies the preparation of the meal. Burger buns, sprinkled with sesame seeds, are easy to find now, and rissoles are delicious on a picnic when stuffed into soft rolls. The flat, unleavened pitta bread is perfect, too, for all sorts of dishes. For me, nothing can beat a thick, warm slice of crusty bread, although I also like plain, buttered noodles as an accompaniment for meatballs.

Children usually love mince (perhaps partly through laziness, because they don't have to chew), which makes it ideal for family meals. Mince dishes are quick and adaptable and an easy way to get children used to new flavours which they profess not to like. But it is most important that mince should not be thought of merely as family food. With very little effort it can be transformed into a sophisticated dish fit for the most formal occasion.

The English tend to think of mince only as beef but there are, as you will see in this book, all sorts of good things which can be made from minced lamb, pork, veal, turkey and chicken. I have also included minced fish because I cannot resist really good fish cakes and featherlight mousselines. If you have scraps of cooked meat left over they can be minced, flavoured and cooked in the many ways suggested in this book. Lean, raw, minced beef need not necessarily mean steak tartare – I have given two original ways to use it as a variation from the famous dish.

The idea of this book was both welcome and natural to me because I have always found minced meat an inspiring and necessary part of inventive cookery. I hope that you will find here plenty of ideas for ringing the changes with mince for any occasion – from family meals to a special dinner party, from a satisfying main course to an appetising snack.

Note on quantities

Ingredients in the recipes are given in both Imperial (oz, pints, etc) and metric (g, ml, etc) measures: use either set of quantities, but not a mixture of both, in any one recipe. All spoons are level unless otherwise stated; metric spoon measures, if you follow these instead, are always level. Egg size, where unspecified, is a medium-large (size 2–3) egg.

MINCED BEEF

'Strange to see how a good dinner and feasting
reconciles everybody.'

Samuel Pepys

BEEF AND MUSHROOM RISSOLES IN FRESH TOMATO SAUCE

Serves 4–5

1 lb (450 g) beef mince

1 medium-size onion,
grated

a handful of parsley,
chopped finely

1 egg, beaten

4 oz (100 g) mushrooms,
chopped small

1 tablespoon (15 ml spoon)
olive oil

salt and black pepper

For the sauce:

1 lb (450 g) tomatoes

2 oz (50 g) butter or
margarine

1 medium-size onion, sliced
finely in rings

2 cloves of garlic, chopped
finely

salt and black pepper

To garnish:

chopped parsley

*Everyone likes these. Easy to prepare in advance,
they can be kept warm in the oven for hours, making
them ideal for a family meal. They go well with peas
and new potatoes.*

Put the beef in a bowl and knead it with your
hands for a few minutes until it is soft and pasty.
Add the onion, parsley and egg. Mix with a
wooden spoon, mix in the mushrooms and
season well with salt and black pepper. Form
into balls each the size of a ping-pong ball.

Heat the olive oil in a large frying pan and fry
the balls over a high heat for a few minutes, just
to brown them, turning carefully once or twice.
Turn off the heat.

To make the sauce, put the tomatoes in a
bowl, pour boiling water over and leave them
for half a minute. Then drain and skin them and
chop up small. Heat the butter or margarine in a
large, heavy saucepan and add the tomatoes,
onion and garlic. Cover the pan and simmer
gently for 5–10 minutes, until both the onions
and tomatoes are soft; then season to taste with
salt and black pepper.

Spoon the rissoles into the saucepan together
with any frying pan juices. Cover the pan and
simmer gently for 20 minutes. Turn into a
serving dish and sprinkle with plenty of chopped
parsley before serving.

Green Dragon Walnut Meatballs
Beef and Mushroom Rissoles in Fresh Tomato Sauce
Little Meatballs in Rich Cheese Sauce

GREEN DRAGON WALNUT MEATBALLS

For the meatballs:

1 large green pepper

1 lb (450 g) beef or pork mince

2 cloves of garlic, chopped finely

3 oz (75 g) walnuts, chopped

1 tablespoon (15 ml spoon) tomato purée

2 tablespoons (2 × 15 ml spoon) soy sauce

1 teaspoon (5 ml spoon) ground ginger

3–4 pinches of chilli powder

1 tablespoon (15 ml spoon) caster sugar

1 tablespoon (15 ml spoon) sunflower oil for frying

salt

For the sauce:

1½ tablespoons (1–2 × 15 ml spoon) soy sauce

4½ tablespoons (4–5 × 15 ml spoon) water

3 teaspoons (3 × 5 ml spoon) wine vinegar

1½ teaspoons (1–2 × 5 ml spoon) caster sugar

4–5 spring onions, chopped finely

This is not a Chinese recipe but the meatballs have a definite oriental character, with their glossy sweet and sour sauce. They are quick to prepare and make an excellent lunch or supper dish served with flat egg noodles and a green salad.

Cut the green pepper in half and take out the seeds and stem. Bring a small pan of salted water to the boil, put in the pepper, cover the pan and boil for 6–8 minutes, until soft. Drain and chop finely. Put the mince in a bowl and add the chopped pepper, garlic, walnuts, tomato purée and soy sauce. Then add the ground ginger, chilli powder, caster sugar and a good sprinkling of salt.

Mix everything well together with a wooden spoon. Then, with wet hands, form the mixture into small balls, each about the size of a ping-pong ball.

Heat the sunflower oil in a large frying pan and fry the meatballs over a low to medium heat, turning to brown all over, for about 20 minutes. Transfer with a slotted spoon to a serving dish and keep warm in a low oven.

Pour most of the fat out of the pan but leave the residue of meat juices. Add the soy sauce, the water and the vinegar. Stir in the caster sugar and dissolve over a low heat. Then bubble fiercely for a minute or two until you have a thick, dark and syrupy sauce.

Remove from the heat and stir in the chopped spring onions. Spoon the sauce over the meatballs and serve at once.

LITTLE MEATBALLS IN RICH CHEESE SAUCE

Serves 5–6

For the meatballs:

12 oz (350 g) beef mince

4 oz (100 g) semolina

2 rounded tablespoons (4 × 15 ml spoon) tomato purée

3 cloves of garlic, chopped finely

2 teaspoons (2 × 5 ml spoon) oregano

1 tablespoon (15 ml spoon) oil or fat for frying

salt and black pepper

For the sauce:

1 oz (25 g) butter or margarine

2 rounded tablespoons (4 × 15 ml spoon) plain flour

1 pint (600 ml) milk

8 oz (225 g) cheese, grated

5 fl oz (150 ml) carton of soured cream

¼–½ whole nutmeg, grated

salt and black pepper

grated parmesan cheese or extra grated cheese

Oven temperature:
Gas Mark 4/350°F/180°C

These beef meatballs are flavoured with tomato, garlic and oregano and then cooked in a golden cheese sauce combined with soured cream. It's a dish you can make well in advance and keep warm in the oven. The sauce goes particularly well with an accompaniment of new potatoes and lightly cooked cauliflower, broccoli or broad beans.

To make the meatballs, put the mince in a bowl and add the semolina, tomato purée, chopped garlic and oregano. Season generously with salt and black pepper and mix thoroughly together. With your hands form the mixture into small meatballs, each about the size of a medium-size marble. Preheat the oven.

Heat the oil or fat in a large frying pan and fry the meatballs over a fairly high heat, turning them continuously for 5–10 minutes, until dark brown all over. Using a slotted spoon, transfer to a fairly shallow ovenproof dish (2-pint/1-litre capacity), such as an earthenware gratinée or flan dish, in which the meatballs cover the bottom fairly loosely.

To make the sauce, melt the butter or margarine in a heavy saucepan. Remove from the heat, stir in the flour and then gradually stir in the milk. Put back on the heat, bring to the boil, stirring, and let bubble, still stirring, for about 3 minutes. Add the grated cheese and stir until melted. Stir in the soured cream and the grated nutmeg and add salt and pepper to taste.

Pour over the meatballs, covering them. Sprinkle the grated parmesan or extra cheese over the top. Cook in the centre of the oven for 45 minutes.

AMERICAN HAMBURGERS

1–1¼ lb (450–550 g) ground beef

2 oz (50 g) rindless, smoked streaky bacon, minced or chopped finely

2 teaspoons (2 × 5 ml spoon) capers, chopped finely

2–4 pinches of chilli powder

1 heaped teaspoon (2 × 5 ml spoon) caster sugar

salt

oil

These hamburgers are given extra flavour by the addition of a little smoked bacon and some capers. Of course, hamburgers taste best when they have the slightly charred flavour of being cooked on an open-air barbecue, but the most important thing is to leave the centre moist and pink. Serve between hot baps or buns with a good mixed salad.

Put the beef, bacon, capers, chilli powder and sugar in a bowl and mix together thoroughly, seasoning with salt to taste. Divide the mixture into four and pat firmly into hamburgers approximately ½ inch (1 cm) thick. Smear all over with oil. Heat the grill to its hottest and put the hamburgers high up under it. Grill for 2 minutes on each side.

MY MOTHER'S STEAK TARTARE

8 tablespoons (8 × 15 ml spoon) mayonnaise (a good commercial kind will do)

1 large onion, chopped finely

a good handful of parsley, chopped finely

2–3 teaspoons (2–3 × 5 ml spoon) capers, chopped finely

lettuce leaves

1 lb (450 g) fresh ground beef

I much prefer this version to the usual recipe. Developed years ago by my mother, it incorporates mayonnaise instead of egg yolks into the raw beef. Use fresh, not frozen, beef for this recipe. Serve it as a first course or as part of a cold meal accompanied by rather thickly cut wholemeal bread.

Mix the mayonnaise with the onion, parsley and capers. Arrange the lettuce leaves on four individual serving plates. Shortly before you eat mix the beef with the mayonnaise mixture and spoon into a pile on top of the lettuce leaves.

STUFFED PEPPERS GRATINÉE

Serves 4–6

*just over 1 oz (25 g) butter
or margarine*

*1 heaped tablespoon (2 ×
15 ml spoon) plain flour*

¼ pint (150 ml) milk

4 oz (100 g) cheese, grated

grated parmesan cheese

12 oz (350 g) beef mince

*2 oz (50 g) fresh
breadcrumbs*

*2–3 cloves of garlic,
chopped finely*

*1 tablespoon (15 ml spoon)
sage leaves, chopped finely*

*2 tablespoons (2 × 15 ml
spoon) tomato purée*

*1 teaspoon (5 ml spoon)
paprika*

1 large onion

2 large tomatoes

*3 medium-size green
peppers*

salt and black pepper

Oven temperature:
Gas Mark 4/350°F/180°C

*This is a delicious variation of a well-known dish.
The pepper 'boats' are stuffed with a rich beef, tomato
and sage mixture and topped with a golden cheese
sauce flavoured with parmesan. They cook in the oven
on a bed of tomato and onion. It is an extremely
popular dish in our family and very good served with
sautéed potatoes and french beans.*

First make the topping. Melt 1 oz (25 g) of the
butter or margarine in a saucepan, remove from
the heat and stir in the flour. Gradually blend in
the milk. Return to the heat and bring to the
boil, stirring all the time. Let the sauce bubble,
still stirring, for 2–3 minutes. It should be very
thick. Then stir in the grated cheese and remove
from the heat. Stir until the cheese has melted
and the sauce is smooth and then season to taste
with salt and black pepper. Stir in a generous
sprinkling of parmesan and leave to cool.

Mix the mince in a bowl with the breadcrumbs, chopped garlic and sage, tomato purée
and paprika. Season very well with salt and black
pepper. Peel and slice the onion very finely in
rings. Pour boiling water over the tomatoes, skin
them and then chop them up into very small
pieces. Spread the onions and tomatoes on the
bottom of a fairly large ovenproof dish and
season with salt and pepper.

Next cut the peppers in half lengthways and
remove the seeds and stalks. Bring a large pan of
salted water to the boil and boil the pepper
halves for 8–10 minutes, just to soften them a
little. Drain them and then spoon the meat
mixture into the pepper halves, patting it down
to fill them tightly.

Lay the peppers on top of the onion and
tomato mixture. Spoon the thick cheese sauce
on top of each pepper, completely covering the
meat. Sprinkle with more grated parmesan and
dot generously with butter. Cook uncovered in
the centre of the oven for 1 hour.

FAR EASTERN PIE

Pictured on page 5   Serves 6

3 oz (75 g) desiccated coconut

1½ pints (900 ml) milk

1 lb (450 g) fresh spinach

2 oz (50 g) butter or margarine

2 rounded teaspoons (3–4 × 5 ml spoon) ground coriander

1 rounded teaspoon (2 × 5 ml spoon) ground cinnamon

1 teaspoon (5 ml spoon) ground turmeric

½ teaspoon (2.5 ml spoon) chilli powder, plus a little extra

4 cloves of garlic, peeled and chopped finely

1-inch (2.5 cm) piece of fresh ginger, peeled and chopped finely (optional)

1½ lb (675 g) beef mince

juice of ½ lemon

1½ oz (40 g) ground rice

salt

Oven temperature:
Gas Mark 5/375°F/190°C

This pie has a real flavour of the East, with its spicy and slightly hot filling of meat and spinach. It has a creamy topping of ground rice cooked in coconut milk with a golden crunchy crust. Serve simply with a salad.

Preheat the oven. Simmer the coconut in the milk for 5 minutes; then leave the pan on one side while you prepare the rest of the pie.

Wash the spinach and pick off the stalks. Plunge the leaves into boiling, salted water just for a minute or so, until the leaves are limp. Drain well, pressing out the liquid, and chop roughly.

Heat 1 oz (25 g) of the butter or margarine in a large frying pan over a medium heat. Add the coriander, cinnamon and turmeric and the ½ teaspoon (2.5 ml spoon) chilli and stir over the heat for half a minute. Then add the garlic and ginger, if used, and stir for another half minute. Add the mince, stirring and breaking it up over a slightly higher heat for about 5 minutes, until browned. Add the chopped spinach. Remove from the heat and stir in the lemon juice. Put the meat in an open, fairly shallow ovenproof dish and put on one side.

To make the topping, put the ground rice in a saucepan and strain in the coconut milk through a sieve, pressing the coconut to extract all the liquid. Leave the coconut on one side for later. Bring the milk and rice to the boil, stirring all the time, and then simmer, stirring a little, for 5 minutes until cooked and thick. If it seems very thick indeed, stir in a little top of the milk. Season to taste with salt and 2–3 pinches of chilli powder. Pour over and spread on top of the meat mixture.

In a small saucepan melt the remaining butter. Remove from the heat and stir in the drained coconut. Spoon this mixture evenly over the rice topping. Cook the pie in the centre of the oven for 40–45 minutes, until richly browned on top.

SURPRISE AVOCADOS

3 avocados

juice of 1 large lemon

1 tablespoon (15 ml spoon) red wine vinegar

2 egg yolks

2 teaspoons (2 × 5 ml spoon) French mustard

a large handful of parsley, chopped finely

2–3 good sprigs of fresh tarragon, chopped finely

1 tablespoon (15 ml spoon) olive oil

12 oz (350 g) ground beef (fresh, not frozen)

1 whole lemon

salt and black pepper

Either as a first course or as part of a cold meal this dish really is a surprise. Under a deceptive topping of plain avocado and lemon slices is a delicious stuffing of puréed avocado mixed with raw ground beef, egg yolks, herbs and mustard. People love it.

Cut the avocados in half and stone. Using a sharp knife, cut a very thin slice off the top of each avocado half, including the skin. Smear at once with a little of the lemon juice to prevent discoloration and leave on one side.

Spoon out the avocado flesh into a bowl and keep the empty shells. Add the remaining lemon juice and vinegar and mash well with a fork. Stir in thoroughly the egg yolks, mustard, herbs and olive oil. Add salt and black pepper to taste. Then mix in the ground beef and check again for seasoning.

Spoon the mixture into the avocado shells and smooth the tops. Lay one of the reserved slices of avocado on each shell. Slice the lemon very thinly and cut into semi-circles. Arrange the lemon slices neatly overlapping in the centre of each avocado over the hole.

Surprise Avocados

SPICY BEEF AND COCONUT CASSEROLE WITH OKRA

Serves 6–8

1 fresh coconut

¾ pint (450 ml) milk

1 oz (25 g) butter

1 tablespoon (15 ml spoon) groundnut oil

2 green chillies, seeds removed under running water and chopped finely

3 cloves of garlic, peeled and chopped finely

2-inch (5 cm) piece of fresh ginger, peeled and chopped finely

1 teaspoon (5 ml spoon) ground coriander

1 teaspoon (5 ml spoon) ground cardamom

1 medium-size onion, peeled and chopped small

1 lb (450 g) minced beef

2 × 14 oz (397 g) can of chopped tomatoes

1 tablespoon (15 ml spoon) tomato purée

2 tablespoons (2 × 15 ml spoon) water

8 oz (225 g) fresh okra

salt

Remember this recipe next time you are lucky on the coconut shy at a fair. It is a useful stew which can be made fairly quickly and then kept warm in the oven for hours. Serve with a green salad.

Bang holes with a skewer in the three points at the top of the coconut and empty out the juice. To break the coconut I find it easiest to throw it down on my stone-tiled kitchen floor, or you can do it with a hammer. When the coconut is broken into several bits, ease the flesh from the shell with a knife. Cut about a quarter of the pieces into very thin slices with a sharp knife. Roughly chop the remaining coconut, put in a food processor or liquidiser with the milk and whizz to a mush. (Or, grate and mix with the milk.) Put to one side.

Heat the butter and oil in a flameproof casserole on top of the stove over a medium heat. Add the chopped chillies, garlic and ginger to the casserole together with the coriander and cardamom. Stir around for a minute and then add the chopped onion and stir for another minute. Turn the heat up and add the minced beef. Dig around constantly with a wooden spoon until browned and separated. Turn the heat to low and add the canned tomatoes and the tomato purée mixed with the water. Cover the casserole and simmer gently on top of the stove, stirring occasionally, for 20–25 minutes.

Meanwhile, cut off the tops of the okra. When the beef is ready, add the okra, cover the casserole again and cook for another 5 minutes. Season to taste with salt. Before serving, pour the coconut mush into a large sieve over a bowl. Press and squeeze the mush with your hands until as much liquid as possible has come out. Just before serving pour this coconut milk on top of the casserole with the coconut slices.

MEAT LOAF WITH BLUE CHEESE FILLING

Pictured on page 5 — Serves 4–5

1 lb (450 g) beef mince

3 oz (75 g) mushrooms, chopped finely

2 oz (50 g) fresh breadcrumbs

4 oz (100 g) streaky bacon, chopped finely

1 clove of garlic, chopped finely

1 small onion, peeled and chopped finely

1 teaspoon (5 ml spoon) oregano or thyme

3 tablespoons (3 × 15 ml spoon) tomato ketchup

1 large egg (size 1–2), beaten

salt and black pepper

For the filling:

4 oz (100 g) Danish Blue cheese

1 tablespoon (15 ml spoon) single cream or top of the milk

1 egg, beaten

a good pinch of chilli powder

3 tablespoons (3 × 15 ml spoon) tomato ketchup

To garnish:

a few sprigs of parsley

Oven temperatures:
Gas Mark 4/350°F/180°C
Gas Mark 9/475°F/240°C

This is a personal variation of the American type of meat loaf – a meal which is easy to make and popular with the whole family. I like a meat loaf to have a rich and definite flavour and in this recipe the blue cheese gives it just that. Try it with baked potatoes, cooked in the oven at the same time, and a green salad or baby carrots.

Preheat the oven to the first setting. In a bowl mix all the ingredients (except those for the filling) together thoroughly and season well with salt and pepper. Grease a 2 lb (1 kg) loaf tin.

Spoon half the mixture into the loaf tin. Crumble the cheese in a small bowl, mix well with the cream or top of the milk and beaten egg and add the chilli powder. Spread this on the layer of meat in the tin. Spoon the remaining meat mixture evenly on top. Bake in the centre of the oven for 1 hour and then remove from the oven.

Turn up the oven to the second setting. Loosen the sides of the loaf with a knife and turn it out very gently on to an ovenproof serving dish. Smear the loaf all over with the tomato ketchup and put back into the oven, cooking for 10–15 minutes. Serve garnished with sprigs of parsley.

SPINACH AND BEEF LAYER PIE

1 lb (450 g) spinach

1 oz (25 g) butter or margarine

1 lb (450 g) beef mince

2 rounded teaspoons (4 × 5 ml spoon) paprika

2 heaped tablespoons (3–4 × 15 ml spoon) plain flour

1 pint (600 ml) tomato juice

grated rind and juice of ½ orange

3–4 pinches of chilli powder

2 large eggs (size 1–2)

2 oz (50 g) blanched almonds, chopped roughly

salt and black pepper

Oven temperature:
Gas Mark 6/400°F/200°C

For some strange reason the flavours of spinach and orange mingle particularly happily together. In this recipe layers of spinach and beef, flavoured with orange and paprika in a tomato sauce, are topped by an egg and crunchy almond mixture. New potatoes go well with this dish.

Preheat the oven. Pull the stems off the spinach. Bring a large pan of salted water to the boil. Plunge in the spinach leaves and boil for 30 seconds, just until the leaves are limp. Drain well, pressing with a wooden spoon to extract all the liquid.

Melt the butter or margarine in a heavy saucepan. Stir in the mince and cook over a high heat, stirring for a few minutes until the meat is well browned. Remove from the heat and stir in the paprika and flour. Gradually add the tomato juice and return to the heat. Stirring all the time, bring to the boil and bubble for about 3 minutes, until thickened. Stir in the orange rind and juice and season to taste with chilli powder and salt.

Pour a thin layer of the meat mixture on the bottom of a greased 2–2½-pint (1–1.4-litre) ovenproof dish. Cover with a layer of spinach and continue with thin layers of meat and spinach, ending with a layer of spinach.

Whisk the eggs, season with salt and black pepper and stir in the chopped almonds. Pour the mixture over the spinach top, spreading it around to cover all the leaves. Cook just above the centre of the oven for 25 minutes.

Spinach and Beef Layer Pie
Old English Lattice Flan
Farmhouse Pie

OLD ENGLISH LATTICE FLAN

Serves 6

1 lb (450 g) potatoes

3 oz (75 g) butter

6 oz (175 g) plain flour

1 lb (450 g) beef mince

4 teaspoons (4 × 5 ml spoon) horseradish sauce

1 medium-size onion, chopped finely

2 tablespoons (2 × 15 ml spoon) tomato purée

2 oz (50 g) seedless raisins, chopped

¼ whole nutmeg, grated

1¾ oz (50 g) can of anchovy fillets

salt and black pepper

Oven temperature:
Gas Mark 6/400°F/200°C

Incorporating the flavours of the seventeenth century and a delicious potato pastry, this pie is an easily made and useful lunch or supper dish. I serve it with a traditional English vegetable such as carrots or cabbage but equally you could accompany it with a salad. It is a pie which is also good eaten cold on a picnic.

Preheat the oven. Boil the potatoes in salted water, drain and mash smoothly, adding the butter. Sift in the flour and stir in thoroughly with a wooden spoon. Gather up the lump of dough and press over the bottom and up the sides of a 9-inch (23 cm) earthenware flan dish.

Put the beef in a bowl together with the horseradish sauce, onion, tomato purée, raisins and nutmeg. Season with salt and black pepper and mix well together. Then spoon the mixture into the dough-lined flan dish. Arrange the anchovies in a criss-cross pattern on top and pour over the oil from the can.

Cook the pie on the centre shelf of the oven for 25–30 minutes.

FARMHOUSE PIE

Serves 5–6

1 lb (450 g) beef mince

1 heaped teaspoon (2 × 5 ml spoon) paprika

2–3 pinches of chilli powder

2 tablespoons (2 × 15 ml spoon) tomato purée

salt

fat for frying

For the topping:

2 oz (50 g) butter or margarine

This is really just a variation of shepherd's pie (ever-popular for family meals) but rather fuller in flavour, with a rich cheese and onion topping instead of the mashed potato. Serve with a green vegetable, buttered carrots or a green salad.

Preheat the oven. Sprinkle the mince with the paprika, chilli powder and salt. Heat a blob of fat in a large frying pan and stir and break up the mince over a fairly high heat until it is separated and sealed. Stir in the tomato purée. Transfer the meat to an ovenproof dish and leave the pan on one side to fry the onions in.

To make the topping, melt the butter in a

2 oz (50 g) plain flour

¾ pint (450 ml) milk

4 oz (100 g) cheese, grated

2 large onions, sliced thinly in rings

salt and black pepper

Oven temperature:
Gas Mark 6/400°F/200°C

saucepan, remove from the heat and stir in the flour until smooth. Gradually add the milk, stirring all the time. Put back on the heat, bring to the boil and bubble gently for 2–3 minutes, still stirring, until thick and smooth. Add the cheese and stir until melted. Season to taste with salt and black pepper and remove the saucepan from the heat.

Heat a little more fat in the frying pan and fry the onion rings over a fairly high heat until soft and golden brown. Stir the onions into the cheese sauce mixture and spoon the topping over the mince.

Bake near the top of the oven for 20–30 minutes, until a rich golden brown.

INDIAN-SPICED MEATBALLS STUFFED WITH CURD CHEESE

Serves 4–5

1 lb (450 g) ground beef

2 teaspoons (2 × 5 ml spoon) coriander seeds

8 pods of cardamom

6–8 cloves

3–4 pinches of chilli powder

3–4 cloves of garlic, chopped finely

1 egg, beaten

4 oz (100 g) curd cheese

1 tablespoon (15 ml spoon) oil

salt

To garnish:

chopped mint leaves or parsley

These aromatic meatballs have a soft filling of curd cheese. They make a good summer meal when arranged on a bed of fresh mint leaves and served with a salad and bread.

Put the ground beef in a bowl and mash with a large wooden spoon until pasty. Grind the coriander seeds, the cardamom seeds (discarding the pods) and the cloves in a coffee grinder or pestle and mortar. Add to the beef with the chilli powder and garlic and season with salt. Thoroughly mix in the beaten egg.

With wet hands, form the mixture into small balls, the size of ping-pong balls, and then flatten them out into circles on an oiled surface. Put a teaspoon of curd cheese on each circle and carefully bring the meat up round to encase the cheese completely, thus making the meatballs larger than before.

Heat the oil in a large frying pan. Fry the meatballs over a medium heat for about 5–7 minutes on each side, until brown. Transfer to a serving dish and sprinkle with the mint or parsley.

THE COMPLETE PICNIC LOAF

1 small white or brown tin loaf

butter or margarine

8 oz (225 g) leeks, washed and trimmed

8 oz (225 g) beef mince

2 tablespoons (2 × 15 ml spoon) tomato purée

2 oz (50 g) cheese, grated

2 large cloves of garlic, chopped finely

2 rounded teaspoons (4 × 5 ml spoon) ground coriander

1 large egg, (size 1–2), beaten

salt and black pepper

Oven temperature:
Gas Mark 5/375°F/190°C

This is a meat, vegetable and cheese loaf cooked within a bread crust. As a balanced meal for outdoor eating, it is convenient, nourishing and sustaining. After cooking it I leave it wrapped in foil and enclosed in an insulated bag. This keeps the heat in well, so that it is still warm when we reach our picnic spot. However, if you prefer to make it well beforehand it is also appetising eaten cold.

Preheat the oven. Cut off one end of the loaf. Pull out all the inside, keeping the empty loaf and cut-off end on one side, and whizz it into breadcrumbs in a liquidiser or a food processor. Heat a good blob of butter or margarine in a large frying pan and fry the crumbs until golden brown and crisp, stirring all the time.

Chop the leeks finely. Put in a large bowl and mix with the minced beef, tomato purée, grated cheese, chopped garlic and ground coriander. Season generously with salt and black pepper and mix in the crisp breadcrumbs and, lastly, the beaten egg.

Spoon the mixture into the empty loaf crust, pressing down slightly but filling right to the brim. Replace the end of the loaf and secure by sticking a skewer through. Smear the loaf all over, especially on top, with about ½ oz (15 g) butter or margarine; then wrap up completely in foil.

Put the foil package in a roasting pan and cook just below the centre of the oven for 1 hour. After cooking, enclose the foil package in an insulated bag to keep hot, if required.

Take a chopping board and a sharp knife on your picnic and cut the loaf into thickish slices just before eating.

The Complete Picnic Loaf
Beef and Onion Flatbreads

BEEF AND ONION FLATBREADS

Serves 5–6

1 large onion

12 oz (350 g) beef mince

½–1 teaspoon (2.5–5 ml
spoon) chilli powder

12 oz (350 g) wholemeal or
85% wholewheat flour,
plus extra for rolling

salt

water

sunflower oil for frying

These are rather like wholemeal pancakes incorporating minced beef and onion. They make a simple meal accompanied by a salad. My children love them for supper, and those who must can smother them with tomato ketchup, too! During the summer they make good picnic food eaten cold and wrapped around a stuffing of lettuce, tomato and fresh mint leaves.

Peel the onion, chop very finely and mix with the mince in a large bowl. Season with the chilli powder and a generous sprinkling of salt. Add the flour and mix it in with your hands. Gradually stir in enough water, a little less than ¼ pint (150 ml), to make the mixture stick together.

Knead on a well-floured board for 3–4 minutes. Then take handfuls of the dough, each about the size of an egg, and shape into round balls. Roll out as thinly as you can, sprinkling both board and rolling pin with plenty of flour to prevent sticking.

Heat about ¼-inch (5 mm) depth of oil in a large, heavy frying pan. Fry the breads one by one at a medium-to-high heat, turning once, until brown on each side. Drain on absorbent paper and pile on a serving dish in a very low oven to keep them warm.

OVENBURGERS

Serves 4

1 lb (450 g) extra-lean
minced beef

a small handful of parsley,
chopped finely (optional)

4 wholemeal baps

3 oz (75 g) Gruyère or
Jarlsberg cheese, grated

This is the simplest way of making a cheeseburger and I think it is one of the best. In the oven the meat is cooked in the bun as the cheese melts on to it. No messy frying or grilling and delicious soft, rare beef. It's a trick to remember for the children's supper.

Preheat the oven. Put the minced beef in a bowl and mix in the parsley, a sprinkling of salt and plenty of black pepper with a wooden spoon.

salt and black pepper

Oven temperature:
Gas Mark 9/475°F/240°C

Cut the baps in half. Divide the meat into four and roughly press each pie on to the bottom half of each bap. Then divide the grated cheese into four and press on top of the mince. Top with the other halves of the baps and wrap the filled baps individually in foil. Put the foil parcels on a shelf towards the top of the oven and cook for 15–20 minutes, depending on how rare you like your meat.

CHILLI CON CARNE EXTRA

Pictured on the back cover   Serves 6

8 oz (225 g) red kidney beans

2 tablespoons (2 × 15 ml spoon) olive oil

2 medium-size onions, sliced in rings

1 lb (450 g) beef mince

2 teaspoons (2 × 5 ml spoon) ground cinnamon

1–3 small, fresh green chillies

14 oz (397 g) can of tomatoes

1 oz (25 g) plain chocolate

2 tablespoons (2 × 15 ml spoon) water

a good handful of parsley, chopped

salt

In Mexico, Spain and in Italy, too, a small amount of dark chocolate is sometimes used in the preparation of savoury dishes. It adds interest, richness and just the right hint of sweetness which spicy dishes often need. There are many recipes for chilli con carne but I like this one, which uses both the chocolate and fresh chillies. One small chilli makes a fairly mild dish which children will eat, but if you prefer a fiery taste increase the number of chillies accordingly. Serve with a green salad and crusty bread.

Soak the beans in water for 8 hours or overnight; then boil them in unsalted water for 1 hour (boiling rapidly for at least 10–15 minutes) and drain.

Heat the olive oil in a large, heavy-based saucepan or flameproof casserole. Stir the onion rings in the oil over a medium heat until soft. Increase the heat, add the beef and dig around for a few minutes until brown. Lower the heat again and add the cinnamon.

Cut open the chillies under running water and remove the seeds; then chop up finely. Add the chopped chillies to the dish together with the cooked kidney beans and the canned tomatoes. In a small saucepan gently melt the chocolate in the water and stir it into the bean, meat and tomato mixture. Season well with salt.

Cover the pan and simmer gently for 1 hour. Check again for seasoning. Before serving stir in the parsley and transfer to a serving dish.

CURRIED BEEF SURPRISE CAKE

4 large eggs (size 1–2)

1 lb (450 g) beef mince

2–3 teaspoons (2–3 × 5 ml spoon) curry powder

2–3 cloves of garlic, chopped finely

1 tablespoon (15 ml spoon) Worcestershire sauce

a handful of fresh mint leaves, chopped finely (optional)

salt

oil

Oven temperature:
Gas Mark 9/475°F/240°C

This easy dish always seems to me to work like magic. The surprise is the running softness of the poached eggs as you cut into the centre of the juicy beef cake. The magic is that the poached eggs retain their softness and don't continue cooking with the beef. It makes a good lunch or supper dish, served with either rice or mashed potato and a green vegetable, or simply with a salad and good bread.

Preheat the oven. Poach the eggs lightly in a poacher until the whites are just set and then plunge them into cold water to cool them and prevent further cooking. Put the beef in a bowl and mix in the curry powder, garlic, Worcestershire sauce and mint, if used. Season with salt.

Spread half the mixture into a 6-inch (15 cm) cake tin (not one with a loose base), pressing it down with a wooden spoon. Then make four depressions in the mince and put in the poached eggs (see diagram). Cover with the remaining mince, again pressing down lightly with a spoon. Brush the top with oil.

Making sure that the oven has reached its maximum heat before putting in the cake, cook towards the top of the oven for 15–20 minutes. Pour the juices out of the tin into a small saucepan and boil fiercely over a high heat for 2–4 minutes until reduced to a syrupy glaze. Turn the cake out carefully and place on a serving dish, top side up. Spoon the reduced juices over the cake and serve.

WELLINGTON PIES

For the pastry:

6 oz (175 g) plain flour

½ teaspoon (2.5 ml spoon) salt

4 tablespoons (4 × 15 ml spoon) olive oil

2 tablespoons (2 × 15 ml spoon) water

For the meat mixture:

1 lb (450 g) lean minced beef

a bunch of spring onions, chopped finely, using as much of the green part as possible

1 teaspoon (5 ml spoon) green peppercorns

4 oz (105 g) can of smoked oysters, drained

salt and black pepper

Oven temperatures:
Gas Mark 6/400°F/200°C
Gas Mark 8/450°F/230°C

These are little open-topped cold pies – suitable for a picnic or a cold meal. They are made with lean beef which is cooked so that it is still pink in the centre. Amidst the meat is a surprise smoked oyster, which imparts a lovely, smoky flavour to the whole pie. The crisp, tasty pastry is made with olive oil.

Oil 8 deep patty tins. To make the pastry, sift the flour with the salt into a bowl. Heat the oil and the water in a saucepan until beginning to bubble; then add the hot liquid to the flour gradually, stirring in with a wooden spoon. Press the warm dough into a ball and then divide into 8 pieces. Press a piece of dough with your fingers into each patty tin to line, bringing the dough up above the edge of the tins. Put in the fridge for a short time and preheat the oven to the first setting.

When the pastry is cold and firm, put the tins just above the centre of the oven and cook for 15 minutes or until golden brown. Remove from the oven and leave on one side while you prepare the filling, turning the oven up to the second setting.

Put the minced beef in a bowl. Add the chopped spring onions and green peppercorns; then season with salt and a little black pepper. Mix thoroughly together with a wooden spoon. Put a heaped teaspoon of the mince mixture into each lined patty tin and then lay the smoked oysters on top, dividing them evenly between the pies. Spoon the remaining mince on top of the oysters to enclose them, heaping the mince up and over them. Cook the pies towards the top of the oven for 10–15 minutes until just browned on top. Leave to cool in the tins and when cold ease the pies out gently with a spatula. Serve cold but not chilled.

KATE'S PIE

Serves 6

a little oil for frying

2 cloves of garlic, chopped finely

½–1 teaspoon (1–2 × 2.5 ml spoon) chilli powder

1 lb (450 g) minced beef

1 tablespoon (15 ml spoon) tomato purée

6 oz (175 g) frozen sweetcorn

4 hard-boiled eggs, peeled and chopped roughly

2 oz (50 g) butter

1 oz (25 g) plain flour

1 pint (600 ml) milk

a large handful of parsley, chopped

8 oz (225 g) packet of puff pastry, thawed if frozen

egg yolk or milk for glazing

salt

Oven temperature:
Gas Mark 7/425°F/220°C

My youngest daughter Kate has always loved pies. For weeks I had been working on recipes for this book and every evening her suppers had been made up of rather exotic experiments. 'I just want a pie' she begged. So I made her this one, a sort of Southern pie; beef with a slight bite of chilli mixed with eggs and sweetcorn, topped with a fresh parsley sauce and puff pastry. She liked it, so did her friends and so did the 'grown-ups'.

Melt a little oil in a large frying pan over a medium heat. Add the chopped garlic and chilli powder and stir; then add the minced beef. Dig around with a wooden spoon until the beef has separated and cooked and any liquid has evaporated. Stir in the tomato purée, remove from the heat and add salt to taste. Add the sweetcorn and chopped eggs. Turn into a 3-pint (1.7-litre) pie or fairly shallow ovenproof dish and pat level. Preheat the oven.

Now melt the butter in a saucepan. Remove from the heat and stir in the flour. Stir in the milk and put back on the heat. Bring up to the boil, stirring, and then bubble, still stirring, for 2–3 minutes. Remove from the heat, add the chopped parsley and season with a little salt. Pour over the mince in the pie dish and leave to cool.

Roll out the pastry to a size big enough to cover the pie dish. Moisten the edges of the dish, lay the pastry on top and cut the edges off. Use the trimmings to cut out decorations. Pierce two holes in the pastry to allow steam to escape and brush the pie with egg yolk or milk. Cook the pie just above the centre of the oven for 20–25 minutes.

LETTUCE PARCELS STUFFED WITH BEEF

Serves 6 (or 8 as a first course)

2 oz (50 g) long grain rice

2 tablespoons (2 × 15 ml spoon) olive oil

1 medium-size onion, chopped

2 cloves of garlic, chopped finely

1 tablespoon (15 ml spoon) paprika

1 lb (450 g) beef mince

2–3 tomatoes, chopped fairly small

4 pinches of chilli powder

½ tablespoon (3 × 2.5 ml spoon) sugar

1 large cos lettuce

salt

For the vinaigrette dressing:

1 tablespoon (15 ml spoon) wine vinegar

3 tablespoons (3 × 15 ml spoon) olive oil

salt and black pepper

Oven temperature (if eating hot):
Gas Mark 5/375°F/190°C

These are delicious hot or cold. Blanched lettuce leaves are stuffed with a tasty beef, tomato and paprika mixture and finished off with a hot vinaigrette sauce; excellent for a hot main dish when served with new or sautéed potatoes and young carrots. Alternatively, the parcels can make a cold first course (and will then serve more) or a cold meal. Garnish with tomato wedges.

Cook the rice in salted water, until just tender, drain and leave on one side.

Heat the olive oil in a large frying pan. Add the chopped onion and fry over a gentle heat, until softened. Then stir in the garlic and paprika. Add the beef and stir and break it up with a wooden spoon over a higher heat for about 5 minutes, until browned. Add the tomatoes and continue cooking, stirring until they are soft and the juices have evaporated. Stir in the cooked rice and season well with salt, the chilli powder and the sugar. Remove from the heat.

Separate and wash the lettuce leaves. Bring a large pan of salted water to the boil and plunge in the whole leaves, just for half a minute. Drain and lay the leaves out on a flat surface. Spoon heaps of the mince mixture on to each lettuce leaf and then wrap up like little parcels.

If eating hot, lay the parcels join side down in a fairly shallow earthenware dish. Cover with foil and heat in the oven for 10–15 minutes. (If necessary, you can keep this dish warm in a low oven for a short time but the leaves will lose their pretty brilliant green, and so it is best to serve it as soon as possible.)

Finally, if serving hot, put the wine vinegar and the olive oil, seasoned with salt and black pepper, in a small saucepan. Heat to bubbling, stir and spoon over the lettuce parcels before serving. If serving cold, mix the vinaigrette ingredients thoroughly and spoon over the cooled parcels.

CRUNCHY STUFFED MEATBALLS

4 oz (100 g) cracked wheat
or couscous

1 lb (450 g) lean minced beef

1 large clove of garlic,
chopped finely

4 tablespoons (4 × 15 ml
spoon) mango chutney

a handful of mint leaves,
chopped

a small handful of parsley,
chopped

1 large egg (size 1–2)

groundnut oil for deep frying

salt and black pepper

I stuff these meatballs with mango chutney, but you can use any kind, and it's even nicer if you have home-made. The meatballs are good for a family meal as children love the cracked wheat coating which combines so well with the soft chutney centre of the meatballs. Serve on a bed of parsley.

Put the cracked wheat or couscous in a bowl, cover with plenty of cold water and leave to soak. Put the minced beef in a bowl. Mix in the chopped garlic and season well with salt and black pepper. Put the chutney in another small bowl and mix in the chopped mint and parsley leaves. Take up enough mince to form into a ball the size of a ping-pong ball and then flatten it in the palm of your hand so that it looks like a small hamburger. Put a blob (a scant teaspoon) of chutney in the centre and then very gently bring up the sides of the meat to enclose it, patting lightly into a ball again. Continue like this until all the mince is used up.

Drain the cracked wheat through a sieve and press out the moisture with a wooden spoon. Whisk the egg lightly in a bowl. One at a time, dip the meatballs in the egg and then in the cracked wheat, lightly patting it on to coat thickly.

Heat fairly deep oil in a large frying pan to a very high heat. Put in the meatballs and fry, turning carefully only once, for 2–3 minutes on each side until light golden brown. Lift out with a slotted spoon and drain on kitchen paper towelling. If possible, eat at once; otherwise keep the meatballs warm in a very low oven for a short time until ready to eat.

Farmyard Pie with Tomato and Herb Pastry
Lettuce Parcels Stuffed with Beef
Crunchy Stuffed Meatballs

FARMYARD PIE WITH TOMATO AND HERB PASTRY

Serves 6

For the pastry:

8 oz (225 g) plain flour

2 large cloves of garlic, peeled

1 teaspoon (5 ml spoon) dried oregano

4 oz (100 g) butter

1 tablespoon (15 ml spoon) tomato purée

2 tablespoons (2 × 15 ml spoon) water

black pepper

For the filling:

1 tablespoon (15 ml spoon) olive oil

1 lb (450 g) lean minced beef or pork

1 large clove of garlic, chopped finely

8 oz (225 g) chicory, chopped small

½ pint (300 ml) milk

2 eggs

1 egg yolk

4 oz (100 g) Cheddar cheese, grated

salt and black pepper

To garnish:

a sprig of basil

Oven temperatures:
Gas Mark 6/400°F/200°C
Gas Mark 3/325°F/170°C

This is a deep, open pie which you make in a loose-based cake tin. It's a good family dish for lunch at the weekend or for supper. Although it looks elaborate, it takes no more time than a shepherd's pie to make. The crisp, flavoured pastry is delicious and a tasty mince and chicory filling is held together with savoury egg custard, topped with melted cheese. Serve simply with a green vegetable or a salad and fresh bread.

To make the pastry, sift the flour into a bowl. Crush the garlic into a small saucepan. Add the oregano, butter, tomato purée, water and a sprinkling of black pepper. Heat gently until the butter has melted, stirring. Pour the hot liquid on to the sifted flour, stirring with a wooden spoon until it sticks together into a dough. Take the warm dough in your hands and press it evenly right up the sides and over the bottom of a lightly buttered 6½–7-inch (16.5–18 cm) deep loose-based cake tin. Refrigerate while you prepare the filling. Preheat the oven to the first setting.

Heat the oil in a large frying pan to a high heat. Add the minced meat and the chopped garlic and stir around for a few minutes until browned all over. Then add the chopped chicory. Stir around, still over a high heat, for another 4–5 minutes. Remove from the heat, season to taste with salt and black pepper and leave on one side.

Put the pastry-lined tin on the centre shelf of the oven and bake for 20 minutes. Remove from the oven, put to one side and turn the heat down to the second setting.

Heat the milk in a saucepan to just below boiling point and remove from the heat. Lightly whisk the eggs and egg yolk in a bowl with a fork, seasoning sparingly with a little salt and black pepper. Pour the hot milk on to the eggs, stirring to mix. Spoon the reserved meat mixture into the pastry case and then pour in the egg mixture – it will seep down a bit. Put back in the oven for 30 minutes; then open the oven door, sprinkle the grated cheese over the top and close the oven door again gently. Continue cooking for 15–20 minutes. (If necessary, turn the oven to the lowest heat and keep warm until ready to eat.) If liked, place under a hot grill for 1–2 minutes before serving.

Loosen the edges of the tin carefully with a round-bladed knife. Put the tin on a smaller tin or mug and push down the sides. Pass a spatula under the bottom of the pastry and gently, as the pastry is crumbly, ease the pie off the base on to a serving plate and garnish with basil.

BEEF AND ANCHOVY MEATBALLS WITH SOURED CREAM

Serves 4–5

3 oz (75 g) white bread, with the crusts cut off

milk

12 oz (350 g) ground beef

1¾ oz (50 g) can of anchovy fillets

2–3 cloves of garlic, peeled

a handful of parsley, chopped finely

flour

1 tablespoon (15 ml spoon) oil

a good blob of butter

5 fl oz (150 ml) carton of soured cream

salt and black pepper

To garnish:

chopped parsley

These meatballs are soft and juicy and none of the gravy runs out while they cook. The anchovy gives them a distinctive and appetising flavour which both adults and children like. Serve them as you like, either with vegetables or just good bread and a salad.

Pull the bread apart roughly and pour over enough milk to soak it. Mash with a fork until pasty. Add the ground beef and drain in the oil from the can of anchovies. With a sharp knife, chop the anchovies and garlic together very finely. Mix into the meat with the parsley and season well with salt and black pepper. With wet hands, form the mixture into meatballs, each about the size of a walnut, and roll in flour.

Heat the oil and butter in a large frying pan. Fry the meatballs over a medium heat for about 6–8 minutes, turning them round all the time, until they are a rich golden brown all over. Transfer to a warm serving dish with a slotted spoon. Stir the soured cream with a fork and spoon over the meatballs. Sprinkle with parsley and serve.

MINCED LAMB

'Oh, where are you going to, all you Big Steamers,
With England's own coal, up and down the salt seas?'
'We are going to fetch you your bread and your butter,
Your beef, pork and mutton, eggs, apples and cheese.'
Rudyard Kipling

When ready-minced and ground lamb are not
readily available, you can buy any lean, boneless
cut of lamb in the amount stated in the recipe and
mince it in a mincer or food processor.

MANTI WITH FRESH TOMATO SAUCE

Serves 6–8

For the manti:

8 oz (225 g) plain flour

1 teaspoon (5 ml spoon) salt

1 egg, beaten

approx. 4–5 tablespoons
(4–5 × 15 ml spoon) water

12 oz (350 g) lamb or veal
mince

1 medium-size onion,
grated

a handful of parsley,
chopped finely

salt and black pepper

For the tomato sauce:

1 lb (450 g) tomatoes

2 oz (50 g) butter

1 clove of garlic, crushed

1 tablespoon (15 ml spoon)
chopped fresh basil or
parsley

salt and black pepper

*You may think that this must be a first cousin of
Italian ravioli but, in fact, it is an ancient Mongolian
dish which is also found in Turkey. It takes time to
make all the little manti but it is quite fun and much
quicker if you can get one of your children or a friend to
do it with you. In any case, it is a dish which can be
prepared ahead and either kept warm or reheated.
And, with the buttery tomato sauce, it is quite
delicious. Serve it simply with a green salad.*

Sift the flour and salt into a bowl. Make a well in
the middle and add the beaten egg. Stir in with a
wooden spoon and add just enough of the water
to form a dough. Gather the dough up with
floured hands and knead well on a floured
surface for 5–10 minutes, until smooth and
pliable. Cover with cling film and leave on one
side.

Put the lamb or veal in a bowl and add the
onion and parsley. Season well with salt and
black pepper and mix together thoroughly.

Roll out the dough on to a large, well-floured
surface as thinly as you possibly can without
tearing it. Then, using a sharp knife, cut it into
1½–2-inch (3.5–5 cm) squares. Spoon a small
teaspoon of the meat mixture into the centre of
each square, moisten the edges and fold over

Oven temperature:
Gas Mark 1/275°F/140°C

corner to corner to make little triangles, and pinch the edges to seal. As you finish the triangles lay them on one side. Re-roll any leftover strips of dough. Preheat the oven.

When all the manti are made bring a very large pan of salted water to the boil. Put in the manti, cover the pan and simmer gently for 15 minutes. Lift out carefully with a slotted spoon and put in a colander. Rinse through briefly with hot water and then turn into a large earthenware dish. Cover with foil and put in the low oven to keep warm while you make the sauce.

To make the sauce, pour boiling water over the tomatoes in a bowl. Leave for half a minute and then drain and skin them. Slice up roughly. Heat the butter in a frying pan and add the chopped tomatoes and garlic. Simmer very gently, stirring once or twice, for 10–15 minutes until the tomatoes are quite soft and mushy. Then stir in the basil or parsley and season to taste with salt and black pepper. Pour the sauce over the manti and serve.

SPRING LAMB PIE

Serves 6–8

1½ lb (675 g) lamb fillet or ground lamb

2 tablespoons (2 × 15 ml spoon) olive oil, plus a little extra

2 large cloves of garlic, chopped finely

2 teaspoons (2 × 5 ml spoon) caraway seeds

1 teaspoon (5 ml spoon) ground cinnamon

1 lb (450 g) cooked beetroot, sliced thinly

5 tablespoons (5 × 15 ml spoon) cornflour

½ pint (300 ml) milk

½ pint (284 ml) carton of soured cream

juice of 1 lemon

1–1¼ lb (450–550 g) baking potatoes, unpeeled and cut into approx. 1–2-inch (2.5–5 cm) slices

salt and black pepper

Oven temperature:
Gas Mark 5/375°F/190°C

Here is an excellent alternative to shepherd's pie: although the flavours are more sophisticated it seems to please both adults and children just as much. It has a certain Russian character, with a layer of beetroot and a soured cream sauce topping the spiced lamb. It has won high marks in our family.

If using lamb fillet, mince or chop in a food processor. Heat the olive oil in a large frying pan to a high heat. Add the lamb and stir around to brown all over; then add the chopped garlic and the spices. Continue stirring around for another minute or two, until any liquid has evaporated. Season with salt and black pepper. Turn the mixture into a large ovenproof gratinée dish and spread level. Arrange the sliced beetroot all over the top.

Now put the cornflour in a saucepan and mix to a smooth paste with 4 tablespoons (4 × 15 ml spoon) of the milk. Gradually stir in the remaining milk and then whisk in the soured cream until smooth. Bring to the boil, stirring all the time with a wooden spoon; then bubble, still stirring, for 3 minutes. Remove from the heat and gradually stir in the lemon juice. Then season to taste with salt and black pepper. Pour this thick sauce all over the beetroot layer in the dish and spread even.

Put the sliced potatoes in a bowl and coat with a little olive oil and salt, using your hands. Arrange the potatoes higgledy-piggledy on top of the soured cream sauce. Bake in the centre of the oven for 1–1¼ hours, until the potatoes are browned and soft when you insert a small knife. Keep the pie warm in a low oven if necessary and serve simply with one green vegetable.

ONION AND YOGURT BUNS STUFFED WITH SPICED LAMB

Serves 6–8

For the filling:

1 tablespoon (15 ml spoon) groundnut or sunflower oil

2 cloves of garlic, chopped finely

1 teaspoon (5 ml spoon) paprika

1 teaspoon (5 ml spoon) ground cinnamon

9 oz (250 g) minced lamb

a little chilli powder

salt

For the dough:

12 oz (350 g) strong plain flour, plus extra for flouring

1 teaspoon (5 ml spoon) salt

2 teaspoons (2 × 5 ml spoon) bicarbonate of soda

2 teaspoons (2 × 5 ml spoon) cream of tartar

2 medium-size onions, peeled and chopped finely

6 tablespoons (6 × 15 ml spoon) natural yogurt

approx. 8 fl oz (240 ml) milk

1 egg yolk, mixed with 1 tablespoon (15 ml spoon) milk, for glazing

Oven temperature:
Gas Mark 6/400°F/200°C

Everyone loves these. They don't take long to make and are perfect to take on picnics or for a snack lunch. If you make them in advance for your picnic, reheat them before setting out and then keep them warm on the journey by wrapping in foil and an insulated bag.

Heat the oil in a frying pan over a medium heat. Add the chopped garlic, paprika and cinnamon and stir around for a minute. Then add the minced lamb, increase the heat slightly and dig around with a wooden spoon for about 5 minutes until cooked and separated. Remove from the heat and season to taste with salt and a little chilli powder. Transfer the mixture to a bowl and leave to cool while you prepare the dough. Preheat the oven.

Sift the flour, salt, bicarbonate of soda and cream of tartar into a bowl. Mix in the chopped onions. Stir the yogurt and the milk into the flour mixture with a wooden spoon to form a dough. (The dough should be quite sticky – add more milk if necessary.) Turn the dough out on to a well-floured surface and, using floured hands, knead lightly.

Take a bit of the dough and shape into a ball the size of a ping-pong ball. Flatten like a hamburger and pile about 2 teaspoons of the mince mixture in the centre. Bring up the sides to enclose the meat and then roll it again lightly to form a ball. Continue like this until you have used up all the dough and mince mixture. Place the buns a little apart on a large, lightly buttered baking sheet. Brush the buns with the egg yolk and cook in the centre of the oven for 20–25 minutes until golden brown.

SPICY MEAT PIES WITH CAPERS

2 tablespoons (2 × 15 ml spoon) sunflower oil, plus a little extra for greasing

3 cloves of garlic, chopped finely

1–2 small fresh chillies, de-seeded and chopped finely

2 teaspoons (2 × 5 ml spoon) ground cinnamon

1 medium-size red pepper, chopped finely

2 tomatoes, chopped into small pieces

8 oz (225 g) lamb or beef mince

1 teaspoon (5 ml spoon) capers, chopped

13 oz (375 g) packet of puff pastry, thawed if frozen

salt and pepper

Oven temperature:
Gas Mark 7/425°F/220°C

These puffed up and crisp little pies have a tasty filling of meat and capers spiced with fresh chilli, garlic and cinnamon. They are good for a light lunch or supper, accompanied by a mixed salad, or you could even pass them around as a heartening snack on a cold day.

Heat the oil in a large frying pan to medium heat. Add the chopped garlic, chillies and cinnamon and stir for half a minute. Then add the chopped red pepper and tomatoes and fry for a minute or two. Finally add the meat and capers and season with salt. Fry over a high heat for 8–10 minutes, stirring until the meat is browned and the juices have evaporated – don't worry if a lot of oil runs out. Check for seasoning and add salt or pepper if necessary. Then spread the mixture on to a plate and leave to become cold. Preheat the oven.

Roll out the pastry to 1/8–1/4 inch (2.5–5 mm) thick. Brush 12 patty tins with oil. Use a 3-inch (7.5 cm) fluted pastry cutter to cut out 12 rounds and then a 2½-inch (6.5 cm) cutter to produce a further 12 rounds. Line the patty tins with the larger rounds. Spoon in the cooled mince mixture, filling the pies to the top. Moisten the edges of the smaller rounds and place on top of the mixture, pressing down slightly round the edges.

Brush the pies with oil and cut a little hole in the centre of each pie. Bake the pies in the centre of the oven for about 15 minutes until well risen and golden brown.

Crispy Lamb and Mint Rolls
Spicy Meat Pies with Capers

CRISPY LAMB AND MINT ROLLS

Serves 5–6

12 oz (350 g) lamb mince

3 cloves of garlic, chopped finely

2 rounded teaspoons (4 × 5 ml spoon) ground cumin

¼–½ teaspoon (1.25– 2.5 ml spoon) chilli powder

a large handful of fresh mint leaves, chopped finely

1 large egg (size 1–2), beaten

13 oz (375 g) packet of puff pastry, thawed if frozen

salt

fat for frying and oil for deep-frying

These can be eaten either as a substantial snack or as a lunch or supper dish accompanied by a salad. They look a bit like sausage rolls, with a much crisper pastry, but their tasty filling of lamb flavoured with fresh mint and cumin makes them far more interesting. You can make them in advance if you like, and either reheat them or keep them warm in the oven.

Mix the lamb in a bowl with the chopped garlic, cumin and chilli powder and season well with salt. Heat a little fat in a large frying pan and fry the mince mixture over the highest heat, stirring all the time, for 5–8 minutes until cooked. Transfer to a bowl and leave to become completely cold. Chop up most of the mint leaves, reserving a few for garnish, and stir into the cold meat mixture with the beaten egg.

Roll out the pastry lengthways into a long strip, about 26 × 8 inches (65 × 20 cm). Cut in half lengthways, to make two long thin strips (see diagram 1). Spoon the meat mixture evenly on to both strips and press down firmly. Roll the strips over widthways, like very long, thin swiss rolls (see diagram 2). Press the edges to seal and cut the two rolls into 2½-inch (6.5 cm) lengths.

Fill a large, heavy-based saucepan with enough oil to deep-fry. Put on a high heat and when very hot add about half the pastry rolls and fry for a few minutes, until puffed up and golden brown. Remove with a slotted spoon and drain on kitchen paper towelling. Fry the remaining rolls. Pile all the rolls up on a plate and serve decorated with the reserved mint leaves.

LAMB AND AUBERGINE DOME WITH FRESH TOMATO SAUCE

1–1¼ lb (450–550 g) aubergines

2 medium-size onions, peeled and chopped finely

a little over 1 tablespoon (15 ml spoon) olive oil

a good knob of butter or margarine

12 oz (350 g) lamb mince

2 oz (50 g) cheese, grated

2 oz (50 g) blanched almonds, chopped roughly

2 large eggs (size 1–2), beaten

salt and black pepper

a sprinkling of flour

For the tomato sauce:

4 tomatoes

1 tablespoon (15 ml spoon) olive oil

1 oz (25 g) butter or margarine

2 tablespoons (2 × 15 ml spoon) tomato purée

3 tablespoons (3 × 15 ml spoon) water

1 rounded teaspoon (2 × 5 ml spoon) sugar

salt and black pepper

Oven temperature:
Gas Mark 5/375°F/190°C

This is a sort of meat and vegetable loaf, with a lovely flavour and soft texture, studded with crunchy pieces of almond. It is served with a brilliant tomato sauce and I like it accompanied by a salad and either boiled potatoes or good fresh bread.

Peel the aubergines and slice into rounds. Rub all over with salt and leave in a colander in the sink for half an hour or more to let the bitter juices drain away. Preheat the oven.

Meanwhile, heat 1 tablespoon (15 ml spoon) of the olive oil and the butter or margarine in a frying pan and fry the onions gently until golden. Leave on one side.

Rinse the salt from the aubergines. Bring a pan of water to the boil. Cover and boil the aubergine slices for only 2 minutes, just until tender. Rinse with cold water, drain and chop up finely. If the aubergines are still hot, let them cool.

Pound the lamb well with a wooden spoon until it is pasty, or whizz it briefly in a food processor. Put it in a mixing bowl and add the fried onions, aubergines, grated cheese and chopped almonds. Season well, add the beaten eggs and mix all together thoroughly.

Spoon the mixture into a shallow, round ovenproof dish and, with wet hands, shape into a smooth dome shape. Smear with the extra oil and sprinkle all over with flour. Cook in the centre of the oven for 1 hour.

While the dome is cooking, make the tomato sauce. Pour boiling water over the tomatoes, drain them, skin and chop the flesh finely. Heat the olive oil and butter or margarine in a heavy saucepan, add the chopped tomatoes and stir over the heat for a minute. Then add the tomato purée, water, sugar and a good seasoning of salt and black pepper. Cover the pan and simmer very gently for about half an hour. Pour into a jug and keep warm until ready to serve.

MOUSSAKA WITH GRUYÈRE CHEESE

Serves 6

1¼–1½ lb (550–675 g) aubergines (approx. 3)

a little lemon juice

2 onions

1 oz (25 g) butter or margarine

1 lb (450 g) lamb mince

1 teaspoon (5 ml spoon) ground cinnamon

2 tablespoons (2 × 15 ml spoon) tomato purée

6 tablespoons (6 × 15 ml spoon) water

a good handful of parsley, chopped

4 oz (100 g) Gruyère cheese, sliced thinly

salt and black pepper

For the topping:

2 oz (50 g) butter or margarine

2 oz (50 g) plain flour

¾ pint (450 ml) milk

a little grated nutmeg

2 egg yolks

2 tablespoons (2 × 15 ml spoon) single cream or top of the milk

salt and black pepper

Oven temperature:
Gas Mark 4/350°F/180°C

This most popular dish, sometimes known in England as 'Greek shepherd's pie', is in fact found all over the Middle East, and the name is not Greek but Arabic. It is a useful dish, which can be prepared in advance and needs only a green salad to accompany it. There are infinite ways of making moussaka. This is my own recipe, in which I just boil the aubergines briefly – frying them can be time-consuming and can also cause too much oil to be absorbed. It is not necessary to peel them, but I think it makes the dish taste more subtle. The thin slices of Gruyère cheese on each layer of aubergine add a delicious and luxurious touch.

Peel the aubergines, slice into ¼–½-inch (5 mm–1 cm) rounds and immediately smear with lemon juice to prevent discoloration. Then rub all over with salt and leave in a colander in the sink for half an hour, to drain away the bitter juices. Preheat the oven.

Peel and chop the onions. Heat the butter or margarine in a large frying pan and cook the onion over a gentle heat until softened. Add the minced lamb and fry over a rather higher heat, stirring and breaking up with a wooden spoon until it is separated and sealed. Stir in the ground cinnamon and a good seasoning of salt and pepper. Then stir in the tomato purée and water, and bubble until the water is absorbed. Turn off the heat and stir in the chopped parsley.

Bring a large pan of water to the boil and empty the aubergine slices into it. Cover the pan and boil for 2 minutes. Drain and rinse in cold water.

In a 2½–3-pint (1.4–1.7-litre) ovenproof dish (a glass one shows the layers attractively) make layers of aubergine slices, mince mixture and Gruyère cheese, starting and ending with a layer of aubergine.

To make the topping, melt the butter or margarine in a saucepan, remove from the heat and stir in the flour. Stir in the milk, gradually at

44

first. Bring to the boil, stirring all the time, and then bubble gently, still stirring, for about 3 minutes. Season lightly with salt and black pepper and a little grated nutmeg. Remove from the heat.

Whisk the egg yolks with the cream or top of the milk and gradually add to the white sauce, stirring in thoroughly. If the sauce is at all lumpy, whisk until smooth and then pour on top of the aubergine and meat layers.

Bake in the centre of the oven for about 45 minutes, until a rich golden brown on top.

ATLAS MOUNTAIN SOUP

Pictured on page 4   Serves 4

4 oz (100 g) dried apricots

2 tablespoons (2 × 15 ml spoon) olive oil

2–3 cloves of garlic, chopped finely

2 teaspoons (2 × 5 ml spoon) ground cinnamon

2 teaspoons (2 × 5 ml spoon) ground cumin

2 teaspoons (2 × 5 ml spoon) paprika

1 lb (450 g) lamb or beef mince

4 sticks of celery, cut into 1–2-inch (2.5–5 cm) pieces

1 large green pepper, sliced in rings

1 lb (450 g) tomatoes, sliced roughly

1 lemon

½ pint (300 ml) water

1 tablespoon (15 ml spoon) sugar

salt and black pepper

This spicy soup, which is more like a stew, is sustaining enough to make a complete meal, accompanied by some good, crusty bread. The meat, combined with spices and with a tang of lemon and apricots, has the flavour of North Africa.

Soak the apricots in water for 2 hours or more and then drain.

Heat the olive oil in a fairly large, heavy saucepan over a moderate heat. Add the garlic and spices and stir for 1 minute. Then add the mince, stirring and breaking it up with a wooden spoon over a slightly higher heat for a few minutes until browned. Add the drained apricots and the celery, pepper and tomato. Shave 10–12 strips of rind off the lemon and add to the soup with the juice of the lemon. Stir in the water and then season with the sugar and salt and black pepper. Bring to the boil, cover the pan and simmer gently for half an hour.

MINCED PORK AND VEAL

'Some hae meat an' canna' eat,
An' some hae nane that want it,
But we hae meat an' we can eat,
An' so the Lord be thankit!'
Old Scottish grace

POTATO CROQUETTES STUFFED WITH PORK

Serves 8

2½ lb (1.25 kg) potatoes,
peeled

2 oz (50 g) butter or
margarine, plus a little extra

1 tablespoon (15 ml spoon)
olive oil

1 medium-size onion,
chopped

8 oz (225 g) pork or veal
mince

2 cloves of garlic, chopped
finely

1 heaped teaspoon (2 × 5 ml
spoon) finely chopped
rosemary

4 oz (100 g) Danish Blue
cheese

1 tablespoon (15 ml spoon)
cream or top of the milk

4 oz (100 g) walnut pieces,
chopped finely

salt and black pepper

Oven temperature:
Gas Mark 5/375°F/190°C

*Coated with crunchy walnuts and stuffed with a tasty
mixture of pork, onion and blue cheese, these
croquettes make a satisfying family meal. Serve them
with a green vegetable, such as broccoli, or a salad.*

Preheat the oven. Boil the potatoes until soft and
then mash until smooth, adding the 2 oz (50 g)
butter or margarine. Season with salt and pepper
to taste.

To make the stuffing, heat the olive oil in a
frying pan, add the onion and fry gently until
soft. Increase the heat, add the mince and the
garlic and stir over the heat for a minute or two
until the meat has separated. Add the rosemary
and transfer to a bowl. Crumble in the blue
cheese and mix well into the meat, adding the
cream or top of the milk. Season with salt and
black pepper.

Take small handfuls of the potato mixture and
form into round balls, each about the size of a
large plum. Form a good hole with your thumb
and spoon in a teaspoonful of the stuffing.
Lightly press the potato round the stuffing to
enclose it.

When all the croquettes are stuffed, roll them
lightly in the chopped walnuts and lay them
close together in a large, shallow ovenproof
dish. Dot the potato croquettes with the extra
butter or margarine and cook in the centre of the
oven for 35–45 minutes, until golden brown.

HOT STUFFED AVOCADOS GRATINÉE

Pictured on page 5   Serves 4

2 medium-size red peppers

4 large cloves of garlic, unpeeled

1 tablespoon (15 ml spoon) lemon juice

1 medium-size onion

2 tablespoons (2 × 15 ml spoon) olive oil

8 oz (225 g) pork mince

1 teaspoon (5 ml spoon) oregano

4 large avocados

3 oz (75 g) cheese, grated

salt and black pepper

To garnish:

sprigs of parsley or watercress

Oven temperature:
Gas Mark 5/375°F/190°C

These are a real treat. There is a lot to be said for serving avocados hot, either sliced and briefly sautéed in butter, to add to other vegetables, or as in this recipe, where they make an unusual main course. Here they are stuffed with pork in a sweet red pepper purée and topped with cheese – decorative and delicious. I would serve them with new or sautéed potatoes and either broad beans, petits pois or just a salad.

First preheat the oven. Cut up the red peppers roughly. Put them in a pan of boiling water with the cloves of garlic, cover and simmer for 10 minutes. Drain, peel the cloves of garlic (they should just pop out of their skins) and put them in a food processor or liquidiser with the red pepper and the lemon juice. Season with salt and black pepper and whizz to a purée. Leave on one side.

Peel and chop the onion. Heat the olive oil in a frying pan and fry the onion until softened. Season the pork with salt and black pepper and add to the pan together with the oregano. Stir and break up over the heat for 4–8 minutes, until the pork is cooked. Then stir in the pepper and garlic purée and bubble for a minute or two more. Check the seasoning (it should be highly seasoned in order to combine well with the bland avocado).

Cut the avocados in half, remove the stones and smear the flesh with lemon juice to prevent discoloration. Put in a shallow ovenproof dish and pile the mince mixture into them, spreading it all over the tops as well as into the cavities left by the stones. Then pile the grated cheese on top of the mince.

Cook in the centre of the oven for 15–20 minutes. Before serving, decorate the dish with sprigs of parsley or watercress between the avocados.

TOMATOES STUFFED WITH PORK AND CHEESE

Serves 4

4 very large (Marmande)
tomatoes

just over 2 tablespoons (2 ×
15 ml spoon) olive oil

2 cloves of garlic, chopped
finely

a sprig of rosemary, chopped
finely

1 tablespoon (15 ml spoon)
sugar

8 oz (225 g) pork mince

2 oz (50 g) Gruyère,
Emmenthal or Jarlsberg
cheese, grated

5–6 fresh basil leaves,
chopped roughly (optional)

salt and black pepper

Oven temperature:
Gas Mark 4/350°F/180°C

Some recipes for stuffed tomatoes give a rather stodgy filling, including breadcrumbs or rice. This is not one of them. These stuffed tomatoes can be served hot or cold, either as a first course or as the main course of a light meal accompanied by rice and a green salad. They really are luscious!

Slice off the tops of the tomatoes and reserve. Scoop out all the seeds and most of the flesh and chop the flesh into small pieces. Salt the insides of the empty tomatoes and lay them upside-down in a colander to drain away the liquid. Preheat the oven.

In a large frying pan heat 1 tablespoon (15 ml spoon) of the olive oil and add the chopped tomato, garlic and rosemary. Bubble over a high heat, stirring all the time, for 4–5 minutes until the sauce is reduced and fairly thick. Stir in the caster sugar and bubble for a minute more. Remove from the heat and season well with salt and black pepper. Spoon the sauce into a bowl and put on one side.

Heat another tablespoon (15 ml spoon) of oil in the frying pan. Season the pork with salt and pepper and fry over a high heat, stirring and breaking up with a wooden spoon for about 5 minutes, until well browned and separated. Stir the fried meat into the tomato sauce. Then add the grated cheese and the chopped basil, if used.

Rinse the salt from the tomato shells and dry with kitchen paper towelling. Place the tomato shells in an open ovenproof dish. Spoon the meat mixture into the tomatoes and then replace the cut-off tops of the tomatoes. Brush the tomatoes all over with a little olive oil and cook in the centre of the oven for 20–30 minutes, until the tomatoes are soft.

Pork Rissoles Stuffed with Fennel
Tomatoes Stuffed with Pork and Cheese

PORK RISSOLES STUFFED WITH FENNEL

Serves 6–8

For the rissoles:

8 oz–1 lb (225–450 g) bulb fennel

1½ lb (675 g) pork mince

4 oz (100 g) fresh white breadcrumbs

finely grated rind of 1 orange

1 good tablespoon (1–2 × 15 ml spoon) chopped fennel or dill leaves

1 large egg (size 1–2), beaten

salt and black pepper

For the sauce:

13 oz (375 g) carrots

¾ pint (450 ml) water

1 chicken stock cube

juice of 1 orange

salt and black pepper

Oven temperature:
Gas Mark 4/350°F/180°C

In this unusual dish the minced pork is subtly flavoured with orange rind and fennel or dill leaves, and there is a lovely surprise as you bite into a tender centre of bulb fennel. The rissoles are served under a brilliant carrot sauce flavoured with orange juice. The result is extremely good. Serve with new or mashed potatoes and a green salad.

Preheat the oven. Cut any long stalks off the fennel bulbs, reserving the leaves for garnish later. Slice the bulbs into ½-inch (1 cm) strips. Steam or boil for a few minutes until tender and rinse with cold water to cool.

Mix the pork mince with all the other rissole ingredients in a bowl and season well with salt and black pepper. Divide the cooked fennel into eight equal piles. Then, with wet hands, divide the meat mixture also into eight equal piles. Still with wet hands, press one pile of meat out flat on a wet board. Lay one pile of fennel on top. Bring the meat up round the fennel and form with your hands into a large, fairly round shape, completely encasing the vegetable. Repeat with the other piles of meat and fennel.

Lay the rissoles in a roasting pan and cover with foil. Cook the rissoles in the centre of the oven for 1 hour, removing the foil for the last 20 minutes to brown them a little.

While the rissoles are cooking make the carrot sauce. Peel a 1 oz (25 g) piece of carrot, cut it into the thinnest possible little strips and leave on one side. Bring the water to the boil in a saucepan, add the chicken stock cube and stir to dissolve. Peel and cut up the remaining carrots, add to the stock, cover the pan and simmer until soft. Add the orange juice and leave to cool a little.

When the rissoles have cooked pour the juices off into a saucepan and boil fiercely for 3–4 minutes, until reduced to a thick, syrupy sauce. Transfer the rissoles to a serving plate and spoon the syrupy sauce over them. Keep warm in a low oven while you finish the carrot sauce.

Whizz the carrots and their stock in a food processor or liquidiser until smooth. Then pour into a saucepan, add the reserved carrot strips, reheat and bubble for 1 minute. Check for seasoning and then pour the sauce over the rissoles. Sprinkle with the fennel leaves.

SPINACH NOODLES WITH VEAL AND SWEETBREAD SAUCE

Serves 4–5

8 oz (225 g) sweetbreads

1 oz (25 g) butter or margarine

6 oz (175 g) veal mince

4–5 tomatoes, chopped small

4 oz (100 g) small mushrooms, sliced finely downwards

a generous sprinkling of chopped fresh basil, dill or tarragon leaves

1–2 pinches of chilli powder

½ pint (284 ml) carton of single cream

10 oz (275 g) flat green (spinach-flavoured) noodles

salt

This recipe is for a rich and creamy sauce with a sophisticated flavour which goes particularly well with the green spinach-flavoured noodles. However, it can equally well be a sauce for other types of pasta. If you can obtain fresh basil it is the best herb of all for pasta, but dill or tarragon will do very well. Serve simply with a green salad and a bowl of grated parmesan cheese to sprinkle over the noodles.

Soak the sweetbreads in a bowl of cold water, changing the water two or three times until they are clear of all traces of blood. Then drain and cut up fairly small. Prepare and set out the remaining ingredients.

Melt the butter or margarine in a large frying pan. Fry the veal mince over a fairly high heat, stirring for about a minute, just to seal. Add the chopped tomatoes and stir for another 2–3 minutes. Then reduce the heat to low and add the chopped sweetbreads. Cook just until the sweetbreads look pale and then stir in the sliced mushrooms and chopped herbs. Season with the chilli powder and salt. Finally, add the single cream and bubble in the pan for a minute. Check for seasoning and add more chilli powder and salt if necessary. Take the pan off the heat and leave on one side.

Put the noodles in a large open pan of boiling salted water and cook for 8–12 minutes, until just soft. Drain and rinse with hot water and put in a warm serving bowl. Reheat the sauce in the frying pan, mix with the noodles and serve.

VEGETABLES IN A PORK CASE

Serves 6–8

For the filling:

2 medium-size green peppers

1 large onion

12 oz (350 g) tomatoes

8 oz (225 g) mushrooms

1 tablespoon (15 ml spoon) olive oil

½ oz (15 g) butter

salt and black pepper

For the pork case:

1½ lb (675 g) pork or veal mince

1 tablespoon (15 ml spoon) tomato purée

2 cloves of garlic, crushed

3 teaspoons (3 × 5 ml spoon) French mustard

1 large egg, (size 1–2), beaten

3 oz (75 g) plain wholemeal or wheatmeal flour

salt and black pepper

Oven temperature:
Gas Mark 3/325°F/170°C

People find this dish intriguing. It is rather like a pie with a crust made of meat instead of pastry. The mixture of vegetables, similar to ratatouille, is encased in minced pork flavoured with tomato, garlic, mustard and rosemary and combined with wholemeal flour. I serve it with fried potatoes and a simple green salad.

Make the vegetable filling first. De-seed the peppers and peel the onion. Chop both up roughly. Pour boiling water over the tomatoes, drain and skin them. Chop the tomatoes and the mushrooms up roughly. Preheat the oven.

Heat the olive oil and butter in a large heavy frying pan. Add the chopped pepper and onion and fry gently, stirring quite a bit until softened. Then add the chopped tomatoes and mushrooms and cook for only a minute more. Season with salt and black pepper, remove from the heat and let the mixture cool in the pan while you prepare the meat case.

To make the pork case, put all the ingredients in a mixing bowl, season well with salt and pepper and mix thoroughly with a wooden spoon. Flour a board and lightly butter an 8½–9-inch (21–23 cm) china or earthenware flan dish. With well-floured hands gather the meat mixture into a ball. Take just under two-thirds of it and press it out with your floured hands on to the board in a circular shape bigger than the flan dish. Line the flan dish with it, pushing it up the sides so that it extends slightly over the rim and spoon in the vegetable filling.

Now make another flat circle with the remaining meat mixture, moisten the edges with a little water and put it on top; press down the edge so that it overlaps a bit, as the meat will shrink slightly while cooking. Brush a little olive oil over the top. Bake the dish in the centre of the oven on a baking sheet for ¾–1 hour. To serve, just cut in slices, as with a pie.

Vegetables in a Pork Case ▶

PORK-STUFFED CHICKEN ROLLS COOKED IN WHITE WINE

Serves 4

8 oz (225 g) pork mince

2 cloves of garlic, chopped finely

2 teaspoons (2 × 5 ml spoon) chopped rosemary

1 tablespoon (15 ml spoon) olive oil

4 large chicken breast fillets

1 egg, beaten

¼ pint (150 ml) dry white wine

1 teaspoon (5 ml spoon) cornflour

a small handful of parsley, chopped finely

salt and black pepper

Oven temperature:
Gas Mark 5/375°F/190°C

These little rolls are delectable. Tender fillets of white chicken breast are wrapped round a stuffing of minced pork with rosemary and garlic and are served under a delicate white wine and parsley sauce. Serve it with new potatoes, when possible, or buttered noodles and a crisp vegetable such as french beans or broccoli.

Mix the pork with the chopped garlic and rosemary and season well with salt and black pepper. Heat the olive oil in a frying pan and fry the pork mixture in it over a fairly high heat, stirring and breaking up with a fork to separate, for about 5 minutes. Transfer to a plate or dish and leave to cool. Preheat the oven.

Skin the chicken breast fillets, cut them in half crossways and lay them spaced apart on a large sheet of oiled greaseproof paper on a firm surface. Put another sheet on top and beat the fillets evenly with a rolling pin or other heavy implement until they are spread out and fairly thin. Sprinkle lightly with salt and pepper.

Mix the beaten egg into the pork mixture and put a good spoonful of this stuffing on each fillet. Roll the fillets carefully over the stuffing and place, join side down, in a fairly shallow ovenproof dish into which the rolls will fit fairly closely. Sprinkle any leftover stuffing around the rolls. Pour over the wine and cover with foil or a lid.

Cook the rolls in the centre of the oven for 30–35 minutes until white and just lightly cooked. Pour all the juices off into a saucepan. Mix the cornflour with a spoonful of water until smooth and stir into the juices in the saucepan. Bring to the boil, stirring, and continue stirring as the sauce bubbles for 2–3 minutes. Check the seasoning and, if the sauce seems too thick, stir in a little water. Finally, add the chopped parsley, spoon the sauce over the rolls and serve.

VEAL AND TUNA CROQUETTES WITH CREAMY CAPER SAUCE

12 oz (350 g) veal mince

7 oz (198 g) can of tuna fish

1–2 cloves of garlic, crushed

a sprig of rosemary leaves, chopped finely

1 large egg (size 1–2), beaten

1 teaspoon (5 ml spoon) green peppercorns (optional)

1 oz (25 g) butter

½ pint (284 ml) carton of single cream

2 rounded teaspoons (4 × 5 ml spoon) capers, crushed roughly

salt and black pepper

To garnish:

a little parsley

The Italians are familiar with the combination of veal and tuna in a delicious dish called Vitello Tonnato – slices of cold veal in a tuna and mayonnaise sauce. These hot croquettes are extremely simple to make and, I think, equally tasty. New potatoes and broccoli, broad beans or french beans go well with the sauce.

Put the veal, the tuna with its juices and the crushed garlic and chopped rosemary in a mixing bowl and season with salt and black pepper. Pound very thoroughly and mix together well with a large wooden spoon. Then mix in the beaten egg and the green peppercorns, if used. With wet hands, form the mixture into small, short sausage shapes.

Heat the butter in a large frying pan and cook the croquettes over a medium heat for about 5 minutes on each side, turning carefully, until golden brown. Remove them with a slotted spoon and put in a heated serving dish.

Pour off the fat from the pan, pour in the cream and heat to just bubbling. Stir in the crushed capers, season with salt and pepper and allow the cream just to bubble for 30 seconds. Then pour the sauce over the croquettes, garnish with a little chopped parsley and serve.

PORK, ONION AND COURGETTE TART

For the pastry:

8 oz (225 g) plain flour

½ teaspoon (2.5 ml spoon) salt

4 oz (100 g) butter or margarine

2 oz (50 g) lard

1 egg

2 tablespoons (2 × 15 ml spoon) cold water

For the filling:

1 lb (450 g) courgettes

1 clove of garlic, crushed or chopped finely

8 oz (225 g) pork mince

1 oz (25 g) butter or margarine

1 lb (450 g) onions, peeled and sliced finely in rings

1 sprig of rosemary, chopped finely

½ pint (284 ml) carton of single cream

2 eggs

2 egg yolks

¼ whole nutmeg, grated

salt and black pepper

Oven temperatures:
Gas Mark 7/425°F/220°C
Gas Mark 6/400°F/200°C

This is a scrumptious, creamy mild tart, perfect for a summer meal or for a party. It is at its most delicious hot but can also be eaten cold. The precooking of the crust over an inverted tin gives it a golden crispness which is well worth the extra effort.

To make the pastry, sift the flour and salt into a bowl. Cut in the butter and lard and crumble with your fingertips until it is like breadcrumbs. Whisk the egg with the water and stir thoroughly into the mixture with a knife. With floured hands, gather into a ball. Wrap in cling film and refrigerate for an hour or more.

Preheat the oven to the first setting. Wash the courgettes and cut, unpeeled, into strips about 3 inches × 1 inch (7.5 × 2.5 cm) long. Cook in boiling salted water in a covered pan for 3–4 minutes. Drain and leave on one side.

Grease the outside of a fairly deep 8½–9-inch (21–23 cm) flan or sandwich cake tin. Roll the pastry out on a well-floured board, into a circle big enough to cover the inverted tin. Place the pastry over the inverted tin so that it covers the base and sides; roll back the uneven edges and press to make a neat edge. Prick the top all over neatly with a fork, piercing right through two or three times to allow the steam to escape.

Place the pastry-covered inverted tin on a baking sheet and bake in the centre of the oven for 10–15 minutes, until pale golden brown. Remove from the oven, leave for a few minutes and then place an ovenproof plate on top and turn over, leaving the pastry case on the plate. Remove the tin and put the pastry in the oven for another 5–8 minutes, to brown the inside. Remove from the oven and turn the oven down to the second setting.

Now prepare the rest of the filling. Mix the

Spiced Pork and Beef Loaf en Croûte
Pork, Onion and Courgette Tart

garlic with the pork and season with salt and black pepper. Heat the butter or margarine in a large frying pan. Add the onions and the minced meat and stir constantly over a medium heat for 8–10 minutes, until the onions are soft. Then stir in the chopped rosemary.

Pour the single cream into a bowl and whisk in the eggs and egg yolks. Add the nutmeg and season with salt and black pepper. Spoon the pork and onion mixture into the pastry case and arrange the reserved courgettes in a close circular pattern all over the top. Pour over the cream and eggs. Cook in the centre of the oven for 35–40 minutes until the cream is just set in the middle.

SPICED PORK AND BEEF LOAF EN CROÛTE

Serves 6

For the pork mixture:

12 oz (350 g) pork mince

8 oz (225 g) cheese, cut into small cubes

2–3 cloves of garlic, chopped finely

2 teaspoons (2 × 5 ml spoon) finely chopped rosemary

1 egg, beaten

salt and black pepper

For the beef mixture:

8 oz (225 g) ground beef

3 sticks of celery, chopped finely

6 oz (175 g) carrots, grated

1–2 tablespoons (1–2 × 15 ml spoon) tomato purée

1½ teaspoons (3 × 2.5 ml spoon) ground cinnamon

2–3 cloves of garlic, chopped finely

Here modest mince is transformed with very little trouble into an impressive dinner party dish. A succulent pork and cheese mixture sandwiches a centre of mildly spiced beef and vegetable, all wrapped in a golden crust of puff pastry. It is full of flavour and unfailingly popular. Serve with a salad or a crisp green vegetable such as french beans, and new potatoes.

Put a roasting pan half-full of water on the centre shelf of the oven and heat to the first setting.

Mix all the ingredients for the pork mixture together thoroughly, seasoning well with salt and black pepper. In another bowl, mix up all the beef ingredients, again seasoning well.

Butter a 2 lb (1 kg) loaf tin. Spoon half the pork mixture into the tin and smooth level. Then spoon in all the beef mixture and level. Finally, top with remaining pork mixture. Cover with a piece of buttered foil, put the tin into the roasting pan and cook for 1–1¼ hours.

When the loaf is cooked, pour the juices from round the meat into a small saucepan and leave on one side. Leave the meat in the tin to cool.

When the meat is cold, or almost cold, roll out the pastry to a rectangle approximately 12 × 10 inches (30 × 25 cm). Trim the edges evenly.

1 large egg (size 1–2), beaten

salt and black pepper

For the pastry:

13 oz (375 g) packet of puff pastry, thawed if frozen

egg yolk or milk to glaze

For the sauce:

1 teaspoon (5 ml spoon) cornflour

a little top of the milk

Oven temperatures:
Gas Mark 5/375°F/190°C
Gas Mark 7/425°F/220°C

Heat the oven to the second setting. Turn the meat out of the tin, place it on the pastry and wrap up like a parcel, moistening the edges to seal. Place in a lightly buttered roasting pan with the sealed edges at the bottom. Roll out the trimmings to cut out leaves, etc., as decoration. Moisten their underside and arrange them on top of the loaf. Cut two small slits to let the steam escape. Brush with the egg yolk (for an extra rich glaze) or milk and bake in the centre of the oven for 20–25 minutes, until golden brown.

To make the sauce, mix the cornflour in a teacup with a little water until smooth and stir it into the reserved meat juices in the saucepan. Bring to the boil, stirring all the time, and bubble for 1–2 minutes until thickened. Add a little top of the milk, stir in and then check for seasoning. Serve in a sauce boat with the loaf.

MY BUBBLE AND SQUEAK

Serves 4–5

1 lb (450 g) potatoes, scrubbed and cut into ½–1-inch (1–2.5 cm) pieces

1 tablespoon (15 ml spoon) olive oil

2 cloves of garlic, chopped finely

1 teaspoon (5 ml spoon) caraway seeds

½ teaspoon (2.5 ml spoon) dill seeds

10 oz (275 g) minced pork

the top half of 1 chinese cabbage, sliced thinly

salt and black pepper

This dish can only be said to be vaguely related to Bubble and Squeak. It is a step up from the school-room dish but still extremely popular with all the family and very useful to make at the last moment for supper. To transform it into an even more 'grown-up' dish stir ½ pint (300 ml) soured cream in at the last moment.

Steam or boil the potato pieces until cooked. Heat the olive oil in a large frying pan to a medium heat, add the chopped garlic and the caraway and dill seeds and stir around. Add the minced pork and dig around for 5 minutes or so until cooked and separated. Then add the sliced chinese cabbage and stir for a minute or two until limp. Lastly, add the cooked potatoes and stir for another minute or so to heat them. Season to taste with salt and black pepper before transferring to a heated serving dish.

VEAL-STUFFED PORK ROLLS WITH LEMON AND PARSLEY SAUCE

Serves 5–6

1 tablespoon (15 ml spoon) olive oil

1 medium-size onion, chopped

2–3 cloves of garlic, chopped finely

2 rounded teaspoons (3–4 × 5 ml spoon) ground coriander

12 oz (350 g) veal or lamb mince

2 medium-size tomatoes, skinned and chopped small

4–6 pinches of chilli powder, or to taste

12 oz (350 g) pork fillet

1 egg, beaten

½ pint (300 ml) water

juice of 1 lemon

2 teaspoons (2 × 5 ml spoon) cornflour

a handful of parsley, chopped finely

salt and black pepper

Oven temperature:
Gas Mark 4/350°F/180°C

Veal-stuffed Pork Rolls with Lemon and Parsley Sauce ▶

These tender little rolls are quite delicious. The pork fillet is flattened until very thin and then wrapped around a stuffing of minced veal and tomato flavoured with coriander and garlic. It is a dish which is equally suitable for a family meal or a dinner party.

Heat the oil in a large frying pan and fry the onion gently, until soft. Then add the garlic and coriander and stir for half a minute. Increase the heat, add the mince and fry, stirring and breaking up with a wooden spoon, until cooked. Lower the heat again and add the tomatoes. Cook, stirring, until the tomatoes are soft and the mixture dry. Season with salt and the chilli powder. Put to one side and preheat the oven.

Cut the pork fillet across into ½-inch (1 cm) slices. Lay the slices, well spaced out, on a large sheet of oiled greaseproof paper. Cover with another sheet of oiled paper. Beat out evenly with a rolling pin, not too hard or the meat will break up, until the pieces are thin and 2–3 times their original size.

Mix the beaten egg into the mince mixture and then spoon the mixture across the middle of each thin piece of pork. Roll the meat up round the mince filling and place the rolls in a roasting pan, join side down. Press any mince that falls out back into the rolls. Pour the water into the pan and cover with foil. Cook in the centre of the oven for 45 minutes.

Using a slotted spoon or fish slice, transfer the rolls, when cooked, to a serving dish. Strain the juices into a saucepan and add the lemon juice. Mix the cornflour with 2 tablespoons (2 × 15 ml spoon) water until smooth and then stir into the stock and lemon juice. Bring to the boil, stirring, and allow to bubble, still stirring, for 2–3 minutes. Season to taste with salt and black pepper, stir in the chopped parsley and pour over the pork rolls before serving.

ROAST CHICKEN WITH VEAL, RED PEPPER AND FENNEL CROQUETTES

Serves 6–8

8 oz (225 g) minced veal

1 large bulb of fennel

1 medium-size red pepper

1 large clove of garlic, chopped finely

2 teaspoons (2 × 5 ml spoon) paprika

1 oz (25 g) ground rice

3–4 pinches of chilli powder

a little olive oil

3½ lb (1.5 kg) fresh chicken

8 fl oz (240 ml) double cream

sea salt and black pepper

Oven temperature:
Gas Mark 6/400°F/200°C

These tasty little minced veal croquettes greatly enhance a roast chicken, making it much more of a special meal. As the croquettes are cooked with the chicken their juices mingle in the pan to make the base of a really delicious sauce.

Preheat the oven. Put the minced veal in a bowl. Cut the feathery green part off the fennel bulb, chop it finely and keep on one side. Take off any tough looking or browned outer parts of the bulb and cut off the top stems. Chop the bulb finely and add to the mince. Then cut open the red pepper, discard the seeds, chop finely and add to the mince with the chopped garlic, paprika and ground rice. Season with salt and the chilli powder and mix all together thoroughly with a wooden spoon. Using oiled hands, form the mixture into small balls the size of ping-pong balls.

Smear olive oil all over the chicken and sprinkle it with sea salt and black pepper. Place in a roasting pan. Cook in the centre of the oven for 1¼ hours, adding the croquettes after 15–20 minutes. Then, using a slotted spoon, transfer the croquettes to a warmed serving dish. Lift out the chicken and empty the juices from inside it into the roasting pan. Transfer the chicken to a carving board.

Stir the cream into the juices in the roasting pan and heat to bubbling on top of the stove. Season to taste with salt and pepper, stir in the reserved chopped green part of the fennel, bubble for a moment more and then pour into a sauce boat to serve with the chicken. (It is quite rich, so only a small amount is needed for each serving.)

STEAMED PORK PUDDING WITH RED PEPPER AND GREEN PEPPERCORNS

2 large red peppers

1 lb (450 g) pork mince

2 large eggs (size 1–2), beaten

2 tablespoons (2 × 15 ml spoon) tomato purée

1 rounded teaspoon (2 × 5 ml spoon) whole green peppercorns

2–3 pinches of chilli powder

a little butter for greasing

5 fl oz (150 ml) carton of soured cream

salt

I find the flavour of this pudding quite delicious. The red peppers are grilled beforehand to add a smoky taste. It is a good change from meat loaf and just as easy to make. Serve it with boiled potatoes to mop up the tasty juices and a green vegetable, such as crisply cooked cabbage.

Cut the peppers lengthways into four and remove the seeds. Lay the pieces skin side up under a hot grill for about 10 minutes, until the skins are completely blackened and blistered. Then, under cold water, peel off the skins. Chop up as finely as possible.

In a bowl, mix the pork thoroughly with the chopped peppers, beaten eggs, tomato purée and green peppercorns. Season well with salt and the chilli powder.

Generously butter a 2-pint (1-litre) pudding basin. Spoon in the meat mixture and smooth the top. Cover the basin with foil and secure with string, also tying on a string handle. Put the basin in a saucepan with enough hot water to come half-way up. Cover the pan and let the water simmer gently for 1 hour (checking occasionally to see that the water is not boiling away).

Remove the basin from the pan and leave to sit for 5 minutes or so. Then turn out on to a round plate – a fairly large one, as the pudding will be surrounded by delicious juices. Just before serving stir the soured cream with a teaspoon until smooth and spoon over the top of the pudding.

EGGS STUFFED WITH VEAL AND RED PEPPER

Serves 4–6

8 large eggs (size 1–2)

8 oz (225 g) veal or pork mince

a large handful of parsley, chopped

1 large red pepper, chopped finely

1 teaspoon (5 ml spoon) paprika

½–1 teaspoon (1–2 × 2.5 ml spoon) chilli powder

16 blanched almonds

a little oil

salt

Oven temperature:
Gas Mark 5/375°F/190°C

These decorative eggs, which have a bite of chilli, are just as good hot or cold, either as a main course or for more people as a first course. If you are serving them hot they go well with rice and a green vegetable; if cold, arrange them on a bed of lettuce leaves.

Preheat the oven. Hard-boil the eggs and pour cold water over them to cool. In a bowl mix together the minced meat, chopped parsley, red pepper, paprika and chilli powder. Season well with salt.

Peel the eggs and cut them in half lengthways. Turn out the yolks into the meat mixture and mix in very roughly. Arrange the halved egg whites neatly in a 9–9½-inch (23–24 cm) flan dish. Stuff the meat mixture into the halved eggs (I find it easiest with my fingers), piling it up. Press a blanched almond on to the top of each stuffed egg and spoon over a little oil. Cook in the centre of the oven for 25 minutes.

Eggs Stuffed with Veal and Red Pepper

PEAR AND PORK PARCELS

Serves 4

8 oz (225 g) minced pork

1 large clove of garlic, peeled and chopped finely

1-inch (2.5 cm) piece of fresh ginger, peeled and chopped finely

1 tablespoon (15 ml spoon) sunflower or groundnut oil

1 tablespoon (15 ml spoon) soy sauce

2 large firm dessert pears

a little lemon juice

8 oz (225 g) very thin rashers of rindless streaky bacon

salt and black pepper

To serve:

lettuce leaves

Oven temperature:
Gas Mark 4/350°F/180°C

Pears work particularly well in savoury dishes. These pears, stuffed with ginger pork and wrapped in bacon, are a wonderful surprise. You can serve them either on their own as a fairly substantial first course or as a light lunch or supper dish accompanied by a mixed salad and fresh, crusty bread.

Preheat the oven. Put the minced pork in a bowl and mix in the chopped garlic and ginger. Season with salt and black pepper. Heat the oil in a frying pan to a high heat. Add the pork and stir around for 5–6 minutes until cooked and slightly browned. Then add the soy sauce and stir around for a minute more. Remove from the heat.

Peel the pears, cut in half lengthways and rub all over with a little lemon juice to prevent discoloration. Carefully cut out the cores to make a proper hollow in each pear half. Now, on a flat surface, divide the bacon rashers into four. Lay out one pile of bacon flat so that the rashers slightly overlap. Lay a pear half in the centre. Spoon a quarter of the cooked mince mixture into the hollow of the pear – don't worry if a little tumbles over the sides on to the bacon (see diagram). Carefully bring the bacon up to enclose the pear and mince and then lay in a roasting pan. Repeat for the other piles of bacon and pear halves.

Cook in the centre of the oven for 20–25 minutes. (If not ready to eat, keep the dish warm in a low oven.) Arrange a bed of lettuce leaves on a serving plate, put on the bacon parcels, spoon any pan juices over them and serve.

SURPRISE BOMBE SURPRISE

15 oz (425 g) can of black cherries

half a Camembert cheese

2 oz (50 g) almonds, in their skins

2 lb (900 g) minced pork

2 large cloves of garlic, peeled and chopped finely

1 medium-size onion, peeled and chopped finely

2 teaspoons (2 × 5 ml spoon) caraway seeds

1 large egg (size 1–2), whisked lightly

1–1½ oz (25–40 g) flaked almonds

2 teaspoons (2 × 5 ml spoon) cornflour

juice of ½ lemon

salt and black pepper

Oven temperature:
Gas Mark 4/350°F/180°C

The first surprise of course is the unfamiliar idea of a Bombe Surprise made of meat. But in the same way as an ice cream bombe hides a mystery interior, the succulent pork, coated with crisp almond flakes, reveals a centre of cherries, melted Camembert and whole almonds. Garnish with cherries if you like.

Preheat the oven. Strain the juice from the cherries into a saucepan and put on one side. Press the stones out of the cherries and put the fruit in a bowl. Cut the half Camembert into 8 pieces and mix with the cherries. Add the whole almonds. Put the minced pork in another bowl and add the chopped garlic, onion and caraway seeds. Season well; then add the whisked egg and stir all together thoroughly.

Pat the mince into a large ball and put in a lightly oiled roasting pan. Cut off the top of the ball and lay on one side. Then, rather like a potter, hollow out the meat with your hands and bring up the sides to form a bowl shape. Spoon the mixture of cherries, Camembert and nuts into the cavity. Then pat out the reserved top piece of meat and lay it on top, pressing it lightly to join with the sides of the 'bowl'. Pat again all over to make as round a shape as possible and then lightly press the flaked almonds all over the meat.

Cook the bombe in the centre of the oven for 1½ hours. Transfer the bombe with a wide spatula on to a serving dish – if necessary keep warm in a very low oven until ready to eat. Pour the pan juices and any residue into the saucepan of cherry juice. Before serving, mix the cornflour with the lemon juice, stir into the saucepan of juices and bring to the boil, stirring all the time. Then simmer, still stirring, for 2–3 minutes until thickened. Check for seasoning, adding more salt and pepper if liked. Cut the bombe into thick slices from the centre, like a cake, and spoon a little sauce over each piece.

CHINESE HEDGEHOGS

7–8 oz (200–225 g) pudding rice

1 lb (450 g) minced pork

2 cloves of garlic

1-inch (2.5 cm) piece of fresh ginger

8 oz (225 g) can of water chestnuts

1¾ oz (50 g) can of anchovies

2–3 pinches of chilli powder

3–4 tablespoons (3–4 × 15 ml spoon) cornflour

salt

To garnish:

a few spring onions, the top halves sliced thinly

The Chinese have the most ingenious ideas with food and this is one of them which I have slightly adapted. A mixture of pork and water chestnuts is formed into balls, studded with rice and then steamed so that everything cooks together. The result looks a bit like white hedgehogs, hence my name for this unusual dish. Serve with soy sauce.

Put the rice in a sieve and rinse thoroughly with cold water; then put in a bowl of salted cold water and leave to soak for an hour or more.

Meanwhile put the minced pork in a bowl. Peel the garlic and ginger and chop them both finely. Drain the cans of water chestnuts and anchovies and chop them both finely, too. Add all four ingredients to the minced pork and mix thoroughly. Season with a little salt and the chilli powder. Form the mixture into balls the size of large marbles.

After soaking, drain the rice thoroughly in a sieve and put in a mixing bowl. Put the cornflour in another bowl and dip the balls in the cornflour to coat them completely. Then, with wet hands, dip the balls in the rice, patting it on to cover the balls closely. Lay the balls slightly apart in a large steamer or in two layers of a smaller steamer. Cover and steam for 30 minutes. Gently transfer the balls from the steamer to a warmed serving plate and garnish the sides of the dish with spring onion flowers.

Italian Moussaka
Chinese Hedgehogs
Surprise Bombe Surprise

ITALIAN MOUSSAKA

2 large aubergines (1½–
1¾ lb/675–775 g)

juice of 1 lemon

1 lb (450 g) minced veal

2 large cloves of garlic,
chopped finely

1 tablespoon (15 ml spoon)
finely chopped rosemary

3 tablespoons (3 × 15 ml
spoon) olive oil

1 tablespoon (15 ml spoon)
soy sauce

1 medium-size onion,
chopped

1–1¼ lb (450–550 g)
medium-size firm tomatoes

2 teaspoons (2 × 5 ml
spoon) caster sugar

1 mozzarella cheese

salt and black pepper

Oven temperature:
Gas Mark 4/350°F/180°C

*There are certain ingredients which seem to represent
the food of a country more than any others. Tomatoes,
mozzarella cheese and veal could only mean Italy and
aubergines always remind me of Turkey, where they
feature on every menu. Here is a different kind of
moussaka made with veal; it has a topping of baked
tomatoes capped with grilled mozzarella cheese. A
good family dish. Garnish with a sprig of basil.*

Peel the aubergines, slice thinly across and put in
a bowl. Sprinkle generously with half of the
lemon juice and rub with salt. Turn into a
colander and leave in the sink for half an hour to
drain away the bitter juices. Meanwhile, put the
minced veal in a bowl, add the chopped garlic
and rosemary and season with plenty of black
pepper.

Heat 1 tablespoon (15 ml spoon) of the olive
oil in a large frying pan to a high heat. Add the
minced veal and dig around with a wooden
spoon for about 5 minutes until any liquid has
evaporated. Add the remaining lemon juice and
the soy sauce. Stir around and then remove from
the heat. Empty the mince into a bowl and keep
on one side. Put another tablespoon (15 ml
spoon) of the olive oil in the pan and turn the
heat down to medium. Add the chopped onion
and cook, stirring around a bit, until soft. Add
the onion to the mince. Now put the tomatoes in
a bowl and pour boiling water over them. Leave
for a moment and then drain, peel and halve the
tomatoes.

Preheat the oven. Rinse the aubergines very
thoroughly to wash away the salt. Drain and pat
dry with kitchen paper towelling. Put half the
sliced aubergines on the bottom of a 3-pint (1.7-
litre) ovenproof dish and sprinkle with black
pepper. Then spoon in the mince mixture,
spread level, lay on the remaining aubergines
and sprinkle with black pepper again. Finally
arrange the tomato halves, cut side down, in

neat circles to cover the aubergines. Brush the tomatoes with the remaining oil and sprinkle evenly with the caster sugar.

Cook in the centre of the oven for 1½ hours. Just before serving slice the mozzarella cheese across thinly and place the slices on top of the tomatoes fanning out like the petals of a flower. Put under a hot grill for 2–3 minutes just to melt the cheese.

ROLLED PORK AND POTATO PIE

Pictured on page 4

Serves 6

1½ lb (675 g) potatoes

3 oz (75 g) butter or margarine, plus a little extra

3–4 cloves of garlic, chopped finely

1 egg, beaten

1 lb (450 g) pork mince

1 large green pepper, chopped finely

2–3 oz (50–75 g) smoked rindless bacon, chopped finely

2 teaspoons (2 × 5 ml spoon) French mustard

a little plain flour

salt and black pepper

To garnish:

sprigs of parsley

Oven temperature:
Gas Mark 4/350°F/180°C

This is a good family dish, equally popular with adults and children. It is made swiss roll fashion, with garlic-flavoured mashed potato encasing a tasty minced pork mixture and then baked until crispy golden. Serve with a green vegetable or simply a salad.

Preheat the oven. Peel and boil the potatoes. Drain and then mash them smoothly with the 3 oz (75 g) butter or margarine. Season with salt and black pepper. Incorporate the garlic and the beaten egg, using a wooden spoon.

Put the pork in a bowl and add the green pepper and bacon. Stir in the mustard and season very well with salt and pepper.

Sprinkle a sheet of greaseproof paper or kitchen foil generously with flour. Spoon the potato on to the paper and, with floured hands, pat out into an oblong about the size of a swiss roll tin. Spread the meat mixture evenly on top. With the help of the greaseproof paper or foil, roll up the pie from the short end like a swiss roll and then slip it carefully off the paper or foil on to a well-greased rectangular ovenproof dish. Criss-cross the top of the roll with a fork and dot all over with the extra butter or margarine.

Cook in the centre of the oven for 1–1¼ hours until the roll is a rich golden brown. Serve surrounded by sprigs of parsley.

71

STUFFED PORK RISSOLES WITH APRICOT AND ONION SAUCE

1 oz (25 g) butter

1½ lb (675 g) fresh apricots, halved, stoned and chopped roughly

2 large cloves of garlic, chopped finely

2 teaspoons (2 × 5 ml spoon) caster sugar

1½ lb (675 g) minced pork

2 rounded tablespoons (3 × 15 ml spoon) chopped fresh marjoram

3 teaspoons (3 × 5 ml spoon) ground coriander

a little oil for greasing

a little plain flour

2 tablespoons (2 × 15 ml spoon) olive oil

1 large onion, peeled and chopped roughly

8 fl oz (240 ml) water

1 tablespoon (15 ml spoon) lemon juice

5 fl oz (150 ml) carton of double cream

salt and black pepper

To garnish:

lettuce leaves

Oven temperature:
Gas Mark 4/350°F/180°C

When fresh apricots first appear in the shops they are usually too hard and rather too tasteless to eat raw. However, when cooked they come to life and it's useful to know of savoury ways to use them as well as sweet. Pork is famous for going well with sweet and sharp flavours and so in these rissoles the apricots are used for the soft stuffing as well as the creamy sauce.

Heat the butter in a frying pan over a medium heat, add half the chopped apricots and the garlic and stir around over a medium to low heat for about 5 minutes until soft and mushy. Then stir in the caster sugar, turn on to a plate and leave to cool while you prepare the rissole mixture. Preheat the oven.

Put the minced pork in a bowl, add the chopped marjoram and ground coriander and season well with salt and black pepper. Divide the mince into four parts and form into large balls. Press the balls out like large, rather flat hamburgers on an oiled surface. Divide the cooked apricots into four parts and spoon each on to the centre of one 'hamburger'. Then carefully draw up the sides to enclose the apricots and pat gently into a ball again. Roll the balls in a little flour and place in a roasting pan. Cook in the centre of the oven for ¾–1 hour until lightly browned.

Meanwhile, start the sauce. Put the olive oil in a heavy saucepan over a gentle heat, add the chopped onion and stir around until softened and translucent. Then add the water, the rest of the chopped apricots and the lemon juice. Cover the pan and continue cooking over a low heat for at least 30 minutes until the apricots have become soft and rather mushy. Then remove from the heat and leave on one side.

When the rissoles are ready, pour the pan juices into the saucepan of onions and apricots.

(If necessary keep the rissoles warm in a very low oven.) Add the cream to the onion and apricot mixture and season to taste with salt and plenty of black pepper. Before serving, reheat the sauce just up to boiling point. Arrange lettuce leaves all round a heated serving dish, pour the sauce into it and place the rissoles on top.

MINCED PORK WITH APPLES AND SPINACH

Serves 4

2 oz (50 g) butter or margarine

12 oz (350 g) pork mince

1 heaped teaspoon (2 × 5 ml spoon) ground coriander

2 medium-size cooking apples, peeled, quartered, cored and sliced

8 oz (225 g) finely chopped spinach, fresh or thawed from frozen

1 teaspoon (5 ml spoon) finely grated orange rind

1 tablespoon (15 ml spoon) caster sugar

1 tablespoon (15 ml spoon) wine vinegar

5 fl oz (150 ml) carton of soured cream

salt and black pepper

This is a quickly made recipe with a mild and unusual flavour. It is a good supper dish and goes well with rice or mashed potatoes.

Heat 1 oz (25 g) of the butter or margarine in a large frying pan or saucepan. Add the pork and stir and break it up with a wooden spoon over a moderate heat to separate and seal. Add the coriander and season well with salt and black pepper. Then add the remaining butter or margarine, sliced apples, chopped spinach, grated orange rind, caster sugar and vinegar. Season again with salt and pepper.

Cover the pan and cook gently for about 5 minutes, until the apples are tender. Uncover, very roughly stir in the soured cream and transfer to a warm serving dish.

PIGLET PIE

1 tablespoon (15 ml spoon) sunflower oil

12 oz (350 g) pork mince

2 teaspoons (2 × 5 ml spoon) ground coriander (optional)

2 teaspoons (2 × 5 ml spoon) French mustard

3–4 tomatoes, chopped fairly small

8 oz (225 g) frozen sweetcorn, boiled until tender

salt and black pepper

For the pastry:

4 oz (100 g) plain flour

1 teaspoon (5 ml spoon) baking powder

a pinch of salt

4 oz (100 g) butter or margarine

6 oz (175 g) cold mashed potato

a little milk for glazing

Oven temperature:
Gas Mark 5/375°F/190°C

Children adore this pie. It has a delicious crust of potato pastry (a good way to use up leftover boiled potato) and is filled with a tasty mixture of pork, tomatoes and sweetcorn, flavoured with mustard and coriander. A perfect family meal. Serve it with carrots or a green vegetable.

Heat the oil in a large frying pan. Season the pork with salt and black pepper and fry it, stirring and breaking it up with a wooden spoon over a fairly high heat, until sealed. Stir in the coriander, mustard and chopped tomatoes and cook more gently, still stirring, for a further 5 minutes. Stir in the cooked sweetcorn and spoon the mixture into a 2–2½-pint (1–1.4-litre) plate or pie dish and leave to cool. Preheat the oven.

To make the potato pastry sift the flour, baking powder and salt into a bowl. Rub in the butter or margarine until the mixture resembles breadcrumbs. Then work in the mashed potato with your hands and knead slightly until you have a smooth dough.

Gather the pastry into a ball and roll out on a floured board into a piece a little larger than the dish. Lay it over the dish and cut off the excess carefully; press this on to the side of the rim all round. Dampen this pastry rim, lay the pastry lid over it and press down to seal. Trim the edges and make cuts round the edge of the pastry with the back of a knife.

Brush the pie with milk and cook in the centre of the oven for 25–35 minutes, until golden brown all over.

MINCED POULTRY AND GAME

'It's a very odd thing –
As odd as can be –
That whatever Miss T. eats
Turns into Miss T.
Porridge and apples,
Mince, muffins and mutton,
Jam, junket, jumbles –
Not a rap, not a button

It matters; the moment
They're out of her plate,
Though shared by Miss Butcher
And sour Mr Bate,
Tiny and cheerful,
And neat as can be,
Whatever Miss T. eats
Turns into Miss T.'

Walter de la Mare

CHICKEN, VEAL AND SWEETBREAD TERRINE

Serves 6–8

8 oz (225 g) sweetbreads

8 oz (225 g) veal mince

12 oz (350 g) skinned chicken or turkey breasts, minced or chopped finely

1 oz (25 g) plain cashew nuts, chopped roughly

1 teaspoon (5 ml spoon) green peppercorns

5 fl oz (150 ml) carton of double cream

butter

salt and black pepper

Oven temperature:
Gas Mark 2/300°F/150°C

This pâté has a luxuriously delicate and subtle flavour and could hardly be easier to make. Serve it on crisp lettuce leaves with toast, either as a first course or as a part of a cold meal.

Soak the sweetbreads in several changes of cold water to get rid of all traces of blood. Then remove as much of the fine skin as possible and cut the sweetbreads up fairly roughly. Put in a mixing bowl and add all the other prepared ingredients, seasoning generously with salt and pepper and mixing thoroughly together with a wooden spoon.

Half-fill a roasting pan with water, put it just below the centre of the oven and preheat. Butter a 1½-pint (900 ml) earthenware terrine or soufflé dish, spoon the meat mixture into it and smooth the top. Put the dish in the roasting pan and cook for 1¾–2 hours. (If you think the top is getting too brown, lay a piece of foil on top.) Cool completely and then refrigerate before serving.

HAM ROLLS STUFFED WITH TURKEY BREAST IN SPINACH SAUCE

Serves 4

12 oz (350 g) skinned
turkey breast fillets

4 oz (100 g) curd cheese

yolk of 1 large egg (size 1–2)

a medium-size bunch of
fresh chives

8 large slices of ham

a little butter or margarine

1 lb (450 g) spinach,
chopped roughly

salt and pepper

Oven temperature:
Gas Mark 4/350°F/180°C

This is a simple, pretty and delectable dish. When I made it for the first time my eldest daughter said 'Oh please, give me more and more'. The delicate flavours mingle beautifully together. Serve with new potatoes, if possible, and baby carrots.

Mince the turkey fillets or chop in a food processor. Mix thoroughly in a bowl with the curd cheese and the egg yolk. Chop the chives finely (I hold the bunch and snip them with scissors) and stir them into the mixture. Season with salt and pepper.

Put a large pan or dish, half-full of water, in the oven just below the centre and preheat.

Lay out the slices of ham and spoon the mixture evenly towards the end of each piece. Roll each up from the shorter end and arrange the rolls closely together in an ovenproof dish. Smear them with softened butter or margarine and cover the dish with foil. Put the dish of ham rolls in the pan of water and cook for 1 hour.

Pour the juices surrounding the rolls into a large saucepan. Cover the dish of rolls again with the foil and keep warm. Cook the spinach in the juices, with the pan covered, until tender. Season with pepper and then purée in a liquidiser or food processor until smooth. If the purée is very thick, add some butter. Spoon the purée roughly over the rolls just before serving.

Ham Rolls Stuffed with Turkey Breast in Spinach Sauce

TURKEY-STUFFED MUSHROOM PUFFS

Serves 4

1 lb (450 g) turkey breast fillets

2 oz (50 g) butter

1–2 green chillies, de-seeded and chopped finely

1 oz (25 g) plain flour

scant 9 fl oz (270 ml) milk

3 oz (75 g) whole hazelnuts

2 teaspoons (2 × 5 ml spoon) chopped tarragon

4 oz (100 g) frozen petits pois

8 oz (225 g) packet of puff pastry, thawed if frozen

4 extra large flat mushrooms

a little butter for greasing

1 egg yolk

salt

Oven temperature:
Gas Mark 7/425°F/220°C

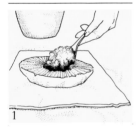

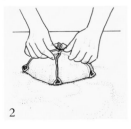

A creamy turkey mixture, tasty with green chilli and tarragon, studded with hazelnuts and petits pois, is stuffed into a large mushroom before being wrapped in puff pastry. The resulting golden parcel makes an individual, exciting meal. I serve it accompanied simply by baby carrots or a green vegetable.

Mince the turkey breasts or chop in a food processor. Melt the butter in a saucepan, stir in the chopped chillies and remove from the heat. Stir in the minced turkey; then stir in the flour and add the milk gradually. Bring to bubbling, stirring all the time with a wooden spoon; then simmer gently, stirring often, for another 10 minutes. Add salt to taste. Then add the hazelnuts and remove from the heat. Stir in the chopped tarragon and the frozen petits pois, turn into a bowl and leave until cold.

Roll out the pastry very thinly into a large piece, as square as possible. Cut the piece of pastry into four rough squares. Cut the stalks off the mushrooms. Lay each mushroom out black side up on a square of pastry and spoon a quarter of the cold turkey mixture on to each one, piling it on (see diagram 1). Bring the corners of the pastry up one by one to the centre top, covering the filling. Moisten the top to seal but don't fold over the sticking-out sides of pastry (see diagram 2). There should be small gaps at each corner of the base so that the mushroom juices can run out. Lay the parcels on a buttered baking sheet. If you have time, keep in the fridge until ready to cook. Preheat the oven.

Brush the parcels all over with egg yolk and cook in the centre of the oven for 20 minutes until a rich golden brown. Transfer the parcels carefully on to a serving plate with a wide spatula, letting any water from the mushrooms run away.

TARRAGON CHICKEN AND MUSHROOM PANCAKE ROULADE

Serves 4–5

For the pancake batter:

1 oz (25 g) butter or margarine, plus a little extra for greasing

1½ oz (40 g) plain flour

a good pinch of salt

1 large egg (size 1–2)

¼ pint (150 ml) milk

For the filling:

3 oz (75 g) butter

10 oz (275 g) skinned chicken breast fillets, minced or chopped finely

1 clove of garlic, chopped finely

2 tablespoons (2 × 15 ml spoon) plain flour

½ pint (300 ml) milk

1 good tablespoon (1–2 × 15 ml spoon) chopped tarragon

2 oz (50 g) small mushrooms, sliced finely

grated parmesan cheese

salt and black pepper

Oven temperatures:
Gas Mark 9/475°F/240°C
Gas Mark 4/350°F/180°C

The combinations of chicken and tarragon and chicken with pancakes are both well known and delicious. In this recipe you simply make one big pancake in the oven (saving a lot of time) and then roll the creamy tarragon chicken mixture up in it like a swiss roll. It is easy, impressive and irresistible. I don't think potatoes are necessary with this – just a green vegetable or green salad, and some good crusty bread for the greedy!

To make the pancake batter, melt the butter or margarine in a saucepan and then cool by dipping into a sink of cold water. Sift the flour and salt into a bowl. Make a well in the flour, break in the egg and add a little of the milk. Mix the egg and milk together with a small whisk or spatula and gradually incorporate the flour, adding more of the milk. Before you have added all the milk beat in the cooled melted butter. Add the remaining milk and whisk thoroughly until smooth and frothy. (Of course, if you have a liquidiser or food processor the batter is made in lightning time by simply whizzing the ingredients all up together.) Leave the batter to stand for half an hour. Preheat the oven to the first setting.

Generously butter a roasting pan measuring approximately 13 × 9 inches (33 × 23 cm). Put the pan on the top shelf of the oven for a few minutes to become hot. Then pour in the batter and cook on the top shelf for 10 minutes, until risen and golden. Turn the pancake out on to a flat surface, cover with a clean damp cloth and leave to cool while you make the filling. Turn the oven down to the second setting.

Melt 2 oz (50 g) of the butter in a heavy saucepan. Add the minced chicken and chopped garlic and stir and break up over the heat for 3–4 minutes; then add the flour and stir in the milk gradually. Bubble, still stirring, for 2–3 minutes, add the tarragon and season to taste with salt and

79

black pepper. Remove from the heat, cool a little and then add the mushrooms.

Spread the mixture all over the cooled pancake and roll up from the short end like a swiss roll. Lay the roll carefully in a shallow ovenproof dish. Smear the top of the roll with the remaining soft or melted butter and sprinkle very generously with grated parmesan. Cook the roll on the centre shelf of the oven for 20–30 minutes.

CHICKEN LIVER, BACON AND AUBERGINE PIE

Serves 5–6

2 large aubergines
(approx. 1¼ lb/550 g)

6 oz (175 g) smoked bacon, with the rind cut off

8 oz (225 g) chicken livers

4 tablespoons (4 × 15 ml spoon) single cream

1 teaspoon (5 ml spoon) oregano

4 oz (100 g) mushrooms, chopped roughly

1 large onion, peeled and chopped finely

butter for frying

oil for frying

1 oz (25 g) fresh white breadcrumbs

salt and black pepper

Oven temperature:
Gas Mark 5/375°F/190°C

This dish has a soft texture and the flavour is rich and tasty. I serve it simply with a mixed salad but for a more substantial meal a dish of rice goes well with it.

Cut the aubergines across into ½-inch (1 cm) slices, rub all over with salt and leave in a colander in a sink for half an hour to drain away the bitter juices. Preheat the oven.

Mince or chop the bacon and chicken livers very finely. Mix in a bowl with the cream, oregano and mushrooms.

Heat a knob of butter in a frying pan and fry the onions gently for 4–5 minutes, until softened. Mix the onions with the bacon mixture and season with black pepper and a little salt.

Thoroughly rinse the salt off the aubergines and dry them. Heat another knob of butter and a little oil in a large frying pan and fry the aubergines in batches over a fairly high heat until golden brown on both sides, adding more butter and oil as necessary. Drain on kitchen paper towelling.

Put half the aubergines on the bottom of an ovenproof dish. Then spoon in the liver and bacon mixture and cover with the remaining aubergines. Finally, sprinkle the breadcrumbs on top and dot with butter. Cook just above the centre of the oven for 25–30 minutes.

Chicken Liver, Bacon and Aubergine Pie
Tarragon Chicken and Mushroom Pancake Roulade
Hunter's Pie

HUNTER'S PIE

For the pastry:

12 oz (350 g) strong white flour

1 teaspoon (5 ml spoon) salt

8 oz (225 g) butter or margarine

2 tablespoons (2 × 15 ml spoon) water

1 egg, beaten

For the filling:

2 wood pigeons

12 oz (350 g) boneless rabbit

8 oz (225 g) veal mince

2 teaspoons (2 × 5 ml spoon) green peppercorns

8–10 juniper berries, crushed (optional)

a bunch of spring onions, cut into ½–¾-inch (1–2 cm) pieces

5 fl oz (150 ml) carton of soured cream

salt and black pepper

To serve:

lettuce or other leaves

Oven temperature:
Gas Mark 4/350°F/180°C

This cold pie, full of flavour, is perfect for parties, picnics or any cold meal, accompanied by a salad. You can make it well in advance but take it out of the fridge an hour or so before you eat, as the rich pastry tastes best when it's not too cold.

To make the pastry, sift the flour and salt into a bowl. Gently melt the butter with the water in a saucepan. Then make a well in the flour and pour in the melted butter and water, stirring into the flour with a wooden spoon as you do so. Stir until evenly mixed and then add the beaten egg. Stir vigorously to a smooth dough. Gather the dough into a ball, wrap in cling film and put in the fridge for at least an hour.

Cut all the flesh you can from the pigeons – I find I can get most of it off by pulling it with my fingers – and cut it up roughly. Mince the boned rabbit or chop in a food processor. Put the pigeon, rabbit and veal in a bowl. Add the green peppercorns, juniper berries, if used, and spring onions. Stir in the soured cream and season with salt and a little black pepper.

Thoroughly butter a 7½–8-inch (19–20 cm) cake tin with a push-up base or a 7-inch (18 cm) pie mould. Take the pastry from the fridge and knead it on a lightly floured board until pliable. Cut off a little under three-quarters of the pastry and roll out into a circle large enough to line the cake tin or pie mould. (If the pastry breaks while you are lining the tin, don't worry, just press it together again.) Spoon the meat mixture into the pastry-lined tin and level the top. Turn back the overlapping edges of the pastry over the edge of the meat and moisten.

Roll out the remaining pastry into a piece big enough to cover the top. Put the cake tin on top of the rolled-out pastry and cut round the edge to make a perfect circle. Carefully place on top of the meat and press down the edges. Prick two or three holes in the pastry with a skewer. Roll out the pastry trimmings to make decorations; dampen and place on top of the pie. (If you have time, put the pie in the fridge for half an hour or more before baking.) Preheat the oven.

Brush the top of the pie with milk and cook in the centre of the oven for 1½–1¾ hours. (Check during the cooking and when the top looks brown enough lay a piece of foil on the top.)

Leave to become cold in the tin. Then carefully ease the edges with a knife and push the pie out. With a spatula, ease the pie off the base of the tin on to a bed of lettuce or other leaves on a serving plate.

TURKEY BALLS WITH LEMON AND CARDAMOM

Serves 4–5

12 oz (350 g) skinned turkey breast fillets

2 oz (50 g) fresh white breadcrumbs

a small bunch of spring onions, chopped finely

finely grated rind of 1 lemon

8–10 pods of cardamom

1 egg, beaten

3–4 pinches of chilli powder

a large knob of butter

1 tablespoon (15 ml spoon) sunflower oil

5 fl oz (150 ml) carton of soured cream

1 tablespoon (15 ml spoon) single cream or top of the milk

salt

To garnish:

a little chopped parsley

These always provoke a rewarding enthusiasm. They have a wonderfully delicate flavour and colour and are always a great success because they are so easy to make. They are a perfect summer lunch dish simply accompanied by salad and some new potatoes.

Mince the turkey fillets or chop them in a food processor. Put in a bowl and mix with the breadcrumbs, chopped spring onions and grated lemon rind. Pop the seeds out of the cardamom pods and crush them finely, discarding the pods. Add to the turkey mixture together with the beaten egg, chilli powder and salt. With wet hands, form into small balls the size of large marbles.

Heat a good blob of butter and the sunflower oil in a frying pan, add the turkey balls and fry over a fairly gentle heat for about 15 minutes, turning several times to cook evenly. Transfer to a warm serving dish and if necessary keep warm in a low oven.

Heat the soured cream with the single cream or top of the milk in a saucepan and spoon on top of the balls. Sprinkle chopped parsley on top and serve.

CLEAR CHICKEN BALL AND WATERCRESS SOUP

Serves 6

10 oz (275 g) skinned chicken breast fillets

2 teaspoons (2 × 5 ml spoon) finely chopped tarragon

finely grated rind and juice of 1 lemon

1 egg white

a bunch of watercress

2 × 14 oz (400 g) can of beef consommé

½ pint (300 ml) water

salt and black pepper

This is a really pretty looking soup and it is simple to make. Glowing white balls of chicken breast, flavoured with lemon and tarragon, float amongst watercress leaves in a clear lemony consommé. You can serve the soup either as a first course or for a light summer lunch accompanied by bread and cheese.

Either mince or chop the chicken breast fillets finely in a food processor. Put in a bowl and add the chopped tarragon and lemon rind. Season well with salt and black pepper and then beat in the egg white thoroughly with a wooden spoon. Using wet hands form the mixture into small balls. Pick just the leaves off the watercress stems and keep on one side. Empty the consommé into a saucepan and add the water. Strain in the lemon juice through a fine sieve and bring to a rapid boil. Then drop in the chicken balls and boil for 4–5 minutes. Meanwhile, pick the watercress leaves off their stems. Add the watercress leaves to the soup, remove from the heat after a second or two and serve.

Clear Chicken Ball and Watercress Soup

Steamed Turkey Balls with Scarlet Sauce

Open Sesame on Emerald Sauce

85

STEAMED TURKEY BALLS WITH SCARLET SAUCE

For the turkey balls:

1½ lb (675 g) turkey breast fillets, skinned

1 oz (25 g) unsalted butter, softened

1 oz (25 g) fresh white breadcrumbs

a large handful of parsley, chopped finely

¼ whole nutmeg, grated

3 tablespoons (3 × 15 ml spoon) freshly grated parmesan cheese

1 egg, whisked

salt and black pepper

For the sauce:

1 medium-size red pepper

1 oz (25 g) butter

1 tablespoon (15 ml spoon) olive oil

2 cloves of garlic, chopped finely

8 oz (225 g) tomatoes, cut small

14 oz (397 g) can of chopped tomatoes

2 tablespoons (2 × 15 ml spoon) tomato purée

salt and chilli powder

To garnish:

whole basil leaves (when in season) and chopped fresh basil or parsley

These are made with turkey breast. Lightly spiced with nutmeg and flavoured with parmesan cheese they make an original change from fried meatballs. The red pepper and tomato sauce is delicious and looks beautiful.

Mince or chop finely the turkey breast. Put in a mixing bowl and add all the remaining turkey ball ingredients. Mix well with a wooden spoon and season generously with salt and black pepper. Using oiled hands form the mixture into small balls the size of ping-pong balls and lay in the top of a steamer. Cover and steam for 20–25 minutes.

Meanwhile, make the sauce. Cut the pepper in half, discard the seeds and chop as finely as possible, in a food processor if you have one. Heat the butter and olive oil in a saucepan, add the chopped pepper and garlic and stir over a medium heat for a minute or two. Then add the fresh tomatoes to the pan and cook for another few minutes until mushy. Add the can of tomatoes and the tomato purée. Cover the pan and simmer gently for another 15–20 minutes. Season to taste with salt and chilli powder. When the turkey balls are ready, pile them on a heated serving plate, spoon the sauce over the top and sprinkle with chopped basil or parsley. Decorate the plate with whole basil leaves.

OPEN SESAME ON EMERALD SAUCE

For the roll:

1 lb (450 g) skinless chicken breast fillets

15 oz (425 g) can of chick-peas

3 cloves of garlic, chopped finely

2 teaspoons (2 × 5 ml spoon) ground coriander

2 teaspoons (2 × 5 ml spoon) dill seeds

3 oz (75 g) butter, softened

2 egg whites

2 oz (50 g) fresh white breadcrumbs

a little olive oil

2 oz (50 g) sesame seeds

salt and black pepper

For the sauce:

2 lb (900 g) courgettes

4 oz (100 g) unsalted butter, cut into pieces

¼–½ whole nutmeg, grated

3–4 pinches of chilli powder

salt

Oven temperatures:
Gas Mark 7/425°F/220°C
Gas Mark 4/350°F/180°C

There's always a lot of guessing about this dish and so far no-one, although ecstatic about the taste, has been able to fathom exactly what it is that they are eating. 'Open Sesame' refers to a sesame-covered roll which is made of delicately spiced chicken breast and chick-peas. Roasted in the oven, it is then cut open and the slices arranged on a bright green sauce – yet another mystery, which is in fact simply a purée of courgettes.

Preheat the oven to the first setting. Mince the chicken breasts or chop in a food processor and put in a bowl. Chop the drained chick-peas to a mush, either in a food processor or by hand. Add to the chicken breasts together with the chopped garlic, ground coriander, dill seeds and softened butter. Season generously with salt and black pepper and then work the mixture with a large wooden spoon until mixed well – it doesn't matter if there are still a few unblended bits of butter. Then add the egg whites and stir in thoroughly. Lastly, stir in the breadcrumbs.

Lightly oil your hands and a board with olive oil and take up the chicken mixture. Shape it into a short, fat sausage shape, about 6 inches (15 cm) long. Then press on the sesame seeds all over the roll, turning it round on the board so that it is densely coated with them. Place the roll in a roasting pan and cook on the centre shelf of the oven for 20 minutes; then turn down the heat to the second setting and cook for 1 hour.

Towards the end of the cooking time, top and tail the courgettes and cut each into 3 or 4 pieces. Boil or steam them for a few minutes until just soft but still bright green in colour. Put in a food processor with the butter, nutmeg, chilli powder and some salt. Whizz until you have a soft purée. Check for seasoning and spoon into a large, open, warmed serving dish. Put the chicken roll on a board, cut into ¼–½-inch (5 mm–1 cm) slices with a sharp knife, arrange them on top of the green sauce and serve.

MINCED FISH

'Fish say, they have their stream and pond;
But is there anything beyond?'

Rupert Brooke

CHEESY FISH CAKES WITH SPRING ONIONS

Pictured on page 4   Serves 4

12 oz (350 g) cod fillets,
fresh or thawed from frozen

3 oz (75 g) fresh white
breadcrumbs

a bunch of spring onions

4 oz (100 g) cheese, grated

1 teaspoon (5 ml spoon)
capers, chopped finely
(optional)

4–5 pinches of chilli powder

1 egg

1 egg yolk

a little plain flour

butter or margarine for
frying

salt

*These light and succulent fish cakes are delicious –
perfect for a light supper or lunch accompanied by a
good mixed salad. For a substantial meal, or when you
are having a cold main course, they also make a good
first course. Some mayonnaise to eat with the hot fish
cakes is excellent.*

If necessary skin the cod fillets (if using frozen
fish this is much easier done before thawing) and
mince or chop in a food processor. Put in a bowl
with the breadcrumbs. Chop the spring onions
finely, using as much of the green stalk as
possible, and add to the fish and breadcrumbs,
together with the grated cheese and the capers.

Season with salt and the chilli powder and mix
all together thoroughly with a wooden spoon.
Whisk the egg and egg yolk and stir into the
mixture. With well-floured hands, shape the
mixture into fairly small fish cakes.

Heat a good blob of butter or margarine in a
large frying pan. Fry the fish cakes (you will
probably have to do them in two batches) over a
medium heat for 5–8 minutes on each side until
golden brown, turning carefully once with a fish
slice. Transfer to a dish, pour over any extra
butter from the pan and serve. (If necessary they
will keep hot in a low oven perfectly well for an
hour or so.)

SMOKED FISH IN TURKEY BREASTS

12 oz (350 g) smoked cod
fillets

3 oz (75 g) fresh white
breadcrumbs

1 teaspoon (5 ml spoon)
chopped dill

finely grated rind of 1 lemon

2 eggs, separated

1 lb (450 g) skinned turkey
breast fillets

5 fl oz (150 ml) carton of
soured cream

2 teaspoons (2 × 5 ml
spoon) tomato purée

salt and black pepper

Oven temperature:
Gas Mark 5/375°F/190°C

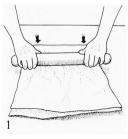

*A delicately flavoured dish, sophisticated in
appearance but simple to achieve. The tender turkey
fillets are beaten out thinly and then wrapped round a
smoked fish filling flavoured with lemon peel and dill.
They are then served under a creamy pink sauce with a
hint of tomato. Delicious with new potatoes and a
green vegetable.*

Skin the fish fillets if necessary. Mince the fish or
chop finely in a food processor. Mix well in a
bowl with the breadcrumbs, dill and lemon
rind. Thoroughly stir in the unbeaten egg whites
and season well with salt and black pepper.
Preheat the oven.

Cut the turkey fillets to give you six equal-size
pieces. Lay them, well spaced out, on an oiled
sheet of greaseproof paper. Lay another oiled
sheet of paper on top. Beat the fillets quite a lot
thinner with a rolling pin or other heavy
implement and then remove the top sheet of the
paper (see diagrams 1 and 2). Spoon the fish
mixture on to each fillet and bring the flattened
fillets up round the fish mixture to encase it as
much as possible (don't worry if there are gaps).
Lay the bundles join side down in a shallow,
buttered ovenproof dish and cover with foil.

Cook in the centre of the oven for half an
hour. Pour off any juices into a small saucepan.
Add the soured cream, the tomato purée and the
egg yolks and stir until smooth. Heat very
gently, stirring all the time and not allowing to
bubble, for 3–5 minutes until the sauce is thick
enough to coat the back of the spoon. Season
with a little salt and black pepper to taste.

Just before serving pour the sauce over the
turkey and fish bundles and sprinkle with a very
little extra chopped dill.

WRAPPED FISH QUENELLES WITH SAFFRON AND VERMOUTH SAUCE

Serves 4

14 oz (400 g) smoked cod or haddock fillets

2 large egg whites (size 1–2)

1 tablespoon (15 ml spoon) chopped fresh fennel leaves

3–4 pinches of chilli powder

4 white, skinned plaice fillets (approx. 12 oz/350 g)

a little olive oil

1 tablespoon (15 ml spoon) cornflour

9 fl oz (270 ml) milk

10–15 strands of saffron

2 large egg yolks (size 1–2)

1 fl oz (30 ml) dry Vermouth

salt

To garnish:

a few leaves of continental parsley or other decorative herb

Oven temperature:
Gas Mark 6/400°F/200°C

I have always loved quenelles. These ones are made of smoked fish, which are wrapped in fillets of plaice and coated with a yellow saffron sauce. It is a delicate dish, lovely in summer accompanied by a young green vegetable and new potatoes.

Preheat the oven. Skin the smoked cod or haddock if necessary and either mince or chop finely in a food processor. Put in a bowl and mix in the egg whites with a wooden spoon. Add the fennel leaves and 2–3 pinches of the chilli powder. Lay out the plaice fillets skin side down. Divide the minced fish mixture into four and pat into fat sausage shapes. Lay one of these on each plaice and roll up loosely. Place in an ovenproof dish, join side downwards, and brush all over with olive oil. Cook the fish rolls in the open dish just above the centre of the oven for 20 minutes.

Meanwhile, make the sauce. Put the cornflour with 2 tablespoons (2 × 15 ml spoon) of the milk in a saucepan and mix until smooth. Stir in the remaining milk and add the saffron. Bring to the boil, stirring all the time, and bubble, still stirring, for 3 minutes. Then remove from the heat and stir in the egg yolks. Add the Vermouth and season to taste with salt and pinch or two of chilli powder. Just before serving pour the sauce over the fish and decorate with a few leaves of continental parsley or other herb.

FISH SAUSAGES IN A GOLDEN SAUCE WITH SPRING ONIONS

Serves 4–5

For the sausages:

1 lb (450 g) cod fillets, fresh or thawed from frozen

2 large egg whites (size 1–2)

½ oz (15 g) cornflour

1 teaspoon (5 ml spoon) baking powder

3 pinches of chilli powder

finely grated rind of 1 orange

salt

For the sauce:

a bunch of spring onions

2 oz (50 g) butter

1 teaspoon (5 ml spoon) paprika

scant 1 oz (25 g) plain flour

¾ pint (450 ml) milk

4 oz (100 g) Red Leicester cheese, grated coarsely

2 large egg yolks (size 1–2)

salt and black pepper

Oven temperature:
Gas Mark 2/300°F/150°C

These are delicate little white fish sausages in a rich, cheesy sauce. You can either serve them as a hot first course, in which case the dish would probably stretch to 8 servings, or as a main course with a crisp green vegetable such as broccoli and with new or sautéed potatoes.

Skin the cod fillets and put in a food processor with the egg whites, cornflour and baking powder. Season with salt and the chilli powder and whizz until smoothly blended. Then stir in the grated orange rind. Using wet hands, take up bits of the mixture and form into small fat sausages. Bring a large saucepan of water to the boil. Drop in the fish sausages and simmer for 7 minutes. Drain in a colander and then put in a rather shallow ovenproof dish. Preheat the oven.

To make the sauce, chop up the spring onions fairly small, using as much of the green part as possible. Melt the butter with the paprika in a saucepan. Remove from the heat and stir in the flour with a wooden spoon until smooth. Stir in the milk, put back on the heat and bring to the boil, stirring. Bubble, still stirring, for about 3 minutes. Add the grated cheese and stir until melted; then stir in the egg yolks. Season to taste with salt and pepper and add the chopped spring onions.

Pour the sauce over the fish sausages. Heat the grill to high and put the dish under it for 2–4 minutes until speckled dark brown. Finally, put the dish on the centre shelf of the oven and cook for 30 minutes before serving.

SMOKED FISH MOUSSE WITH PRAWN SAUCE

For the mousse:

a little butter

½–1 oz (15–25 g) peeled prawns, fresh or thawed from frozen

1 lb (450 g) smoked fish fillets, skinned

whites of 3 large eggs (size 1–2)

½ pint (284 ml) carton of double or single cream

3–4 pinches of chilli powder

salt

For the sauce:

4 oz (100 g) butter

1 scant tablespoon (15 ml spoon) plain flour

½ pint (300 ml) milk

yolks of 3 large eggs (size 1–2), whisked lightly

4 oz (100 g) peeled prawns

1 teaspoon (5 ml spoon) tomato purée

a sprinkling of chopped dill or fennel leaves

2–3 teaspoons (2–3 × 5 ml spoon) white wine vinegar

chilli powder

salt

Oven temperature:
Gas Mark 4/350°F/180°C

Smoked Fish Mousse with Prawn Sauce
Fish Mousselines in Green Pea Sauce ▶

Minced fish instead of meat produces this easily made, pretty, primrose-yellow mousse. It has the most delicate flavour and consistency, combined with a rich and delicious sauce. It is served hot, either as a sustaining first course or as a main course accompanied by new potatoes and a green vegetable, such as broad beans or broccoli.

Put a roasting pan half-full of hot water on the centre shelf of the oven and preheat. Generously smear a 1½–2-pint (900 ml–1-litre) ring mould or cake tin with butter. Arrange some prawns in a circle on the bottom of the tin. Either mince the fish fillets and then pound in a mortar until soft and pasty or whizz in a food processor. Add the unbeaten egg whites and mix in thoroughly. Then mix in the cream and season with chilli powder and salt.

Spoon the fish mixture into the mould or tin and spread evenly. Place in the pan of water in the oven and cook for 20–25 minutes, until firm. (If you have not made the sauce while the mousse was cooking you can switch off the oven and the mousse will stay warm sitting in the pan of water.)

To make the sauce, melt 1 oz (25 g) of the butter in a saucepan. Remove from the heat and stir in the flour. Gradually stir in the milk. Return to the heat and, stirring all the time, bring to the boil and allow to bubble for 2–3 minutes, until thickened and smooth. Stir in the remaining 3 oz (75 g) butter, a little at a time. Then add the egg yolks, prawns and tomato purée, a good sprinkling of chopped dill or fennel leaves and the wine vinegar. Season to taste with salt and chilli powder.

To serve, loosen the edges of the mousse carefully, with a knife if necessary, and turn out on to a serving plate. Pour the sauce into a sauce boat to accompany the mousse.

FISH MOUSSELINES IN GREEN PEA SAUCE

Serves 4

For the mousselines:

8 oz (225 g) smoked, skinned fish fillets, minced or chopped finely in a food processor

4 oz (100 g) cheese, grated finely

whites of 3 large eggs (size 1–2)

3 tablespoons (3 × 15 ml spoon) double or single cream

¼ whole nutmeg, grated

2–3 good pinches of chilli powder

a little plain flour

salt

For the sauce:

8 oz (225 g) green peas, fresh or frozen

yolks of 3 large eggs (size 1–2)

½ pint (300 ml) milk

salt and black pepper

To garnish:

chopped parsley, dill or fennel leaves

This is a most delicate and dreamy dish. A mixture of minced smoked fish, grated cheese and egg whites is dropped spoon by spoon into boiling water resulting in lightly puffed, irregular-shaped balls. These are then enveloped in a luscious green sauce thickened and enriched by the egg yolks. Serve the mousselines either as a hot first course or as a main course accompanied by new potatoes and a tomato salad.

Put the minced fish in a bowl and pound vigorously with a large wooden spoon until pasty. Mash in the grated cheese. Thoroughly mix in the egg whites, one at a time, and then stir in the cream. Season with the nutmeg, chilli powder and salt and leave on one side while the water heats up.

Bring a large saucepan of water to a slow boil. Take teaspoons of the fish mixture and push them off the spoon on to a floured board. Roll in flour and drop them into the water. When all the mixture has been used up continue boiling for 3–4 minutes. Then carefully drain the mousselines in a colander. Put them in a warm serving dish, cover loosely with foil and keep warm in a low oven while you make the sauce.

For the sauce, cook the peas, drain in a sieve and rinse with cold water to cool slightly. Then put them in a liquidiser with the egg yolks and the milk. Whizz until smooth and then pour into a saucepan and heat gently, stirring all the time and not allowing to boil, until thickened. (This usually takes about 5 minutes. If by mistake the sauce should boil, and thus curdle, let it cool slightly, put it back in the liquidiser and whizz for a moment until amalgamated once more.) Season to taste. Pour the sauce over the mousselines, sprinkle with the chopped parsley, dill or fennel leaves and serve.

INDEX TO RECIPES

Design and layout: Ken Vail Graphic Design
Photography: John Lee
Food preparation for photography: Ann Page-Wood
Illustrations: Mandy Doyle
Typesetting: Westholme Graphics Ltd
Printed and bound by Balding & Mansell Ltd,
Wisbech, Cambs